D0876843

THE FRENCH INVASION

OF

WESTERN PENNSYLVANIA

1753

By DONALD H. KENT

COMMONWEALTH OF PENNSYLVANIA

PENNSYLVANIA HISTORICAL AND MUSEUM COMMISSION

HARRISBURG

THE PENNSYLVANIA HISTORICAL AND MUSEUM COMMISSION

ISBN 0-911124-54-3

First Printing, 1954
Third Printing, 1991

CONTENTS

ILLUSTRATIONS

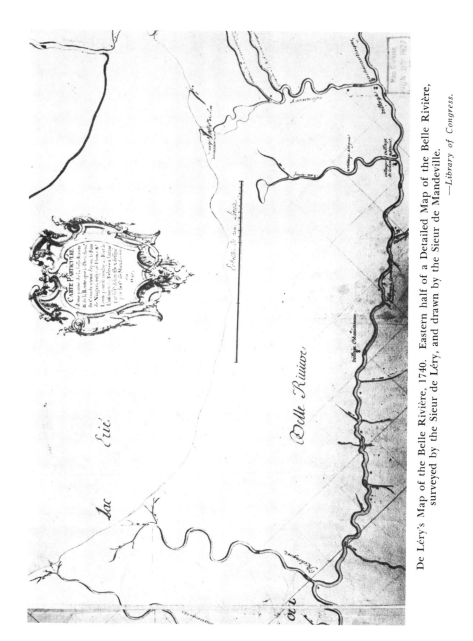

De Léry's Map of the Belle Rivière, 1740. Eastern half of a Detailed Map of the Belle Rivière, surveyed by the Sieur de Léry, and drawn by the Sieur de Mandeville.

—*Library of Congress.*

INTRODUCTION

Two hundred years ago, in the middle years of the eighteenth century, the rival colonial powers of France and Great Britain began to dispute the ownership of the Ohio country, which included what is now western Pennsylvania. French empire-builders felt that their colonies of Canada and Louisiana, to be secure and self-sustaining, must be linked together by the Ohio River. To the British colonies, and particularly to Pennsylvania and Virginia, the Ohio country was a natural area for expansion by trade and settlement. Both sides sent traders and agents to the region, competing for the furs and for the good will of its Indian inhabitants.

In 1753, realizing that peaceful methods of trade and diplomacy were ineffectual, the French sent armed forces from Canada to occupy the Ohio country and fortify its key points. This was a direct threat to the security and expansion of Pennsylvania and other British colonies. It was an invasion of Pennsylvania in terms of the boundaries assigned in her Charter, and also in terms of her present-day boundaries. Of course, Pennsylvania law did not yet run in the territory beyond the mountains, no Pennsylvanian witnessed the landing at Presque Isle in May of 1753, and the Governor in Philadelphia had only vague and indefinite notions of what was happening in a remote corner of his colony. The French invasion was not to become pressing and actual to the people of Pennsylvania until years later, after the outbreak of open warfare, when Indian raiders were sent by the French to ravage the frontier settlements.

This French invasion was not only a major episode in Pennsylvania history; it was also involved in a sequence of events leading to a world war known in America as the French and Indian War, and in Europe as the Seven Years' War. While the French were making their bid for control of the Ohio, the imperial interests of Britain and France were clashing all over the world, near at hand among the Indians of the Miami River, farther away in Acadia and the Lake Champlain region, and on the opposite side of the world in India. Europe, of course, was still the main scene of events, and it was not until French and British diplomats had exchanged complaints and found suitable military allies—not until France by a "diplomatic revolution" had won Austria as a partner, while Britain gained the Prussia of Frederick the Great—that war was formally declared in 1756,

1

long after fighting had begun overseas. With all this tangled and complex skein of causes, it cannot be said that the French invasion of western Pennsylvania caused the Seven Years' War. But, after the French invaded British-claimed territory, war could be taken for granted, sooner or later.

The conflict over the Ohio marked the entrance of western Pennsylvania into world history. The civilized world had known of it but vaguely, as scattered bits of information drifted out from Indian traders and agents. This rich and smiling land drained by the Ohio and its great tributaries, the Allegheny and the Monongahela, now came into the full light of history. It became a stage where events took place affecting the whole civilized world; and names like Buckaloons, Venango, Presque Isle, Le Boeuf, the Forks of the Ohio, Logstown, and the Great Meadows were soon on the maps published by Messrs. Bellin, Scull, and Evans for the information of the public of Paris, London, and Philadelphia.

The French occupation of the Ohio country was a turning point in the history of Pennsylvania, marking the end of the period of peaceful development. None of the earlier colonial wars had actually touched the colony which William Penn and the Friends had nurtured in ways of peace. Now the French thrust for the Ohio threatened the peaceful Province, and in a few years Pennsylvania was to be directly involved in war.

The story of the French invasion of Pennsylvania in 1753 is presented entirely from French sources, so far as possible. The chief exceptions to this rule, the Deposition of Stephen Coffin and George Washington's Journal for 1753, have been used mainly to supplement the French materials. Other than this, only the most casual use of British sources has been made. This seeming neglect finds justification in the fact that, until Washington's visit to Fort Le Boeuf in December, 1753, all the details of the French operations were hidden from the British by a "wilderness curtain." Now, in the two hundredth year since the French army landed at Presque Isle, the curtain can be lifted, thanks to the important French sources which have become accessible in the past few years; and details and particulars can be made clear which were unknown to Pennsylvanians of an earlier day.

2

THE OHIO COUNTRY ATTRACTS ATTENTION

For a long time, while other regions of America were being claimed, annexed, and settled by the nations of Europe, the Ohio valley remained a "forgotten corner."[1] It was not until the middle years of the eighteenth century that Britain and France began to be concerned about this great region.

As the middle British colonies began to develop a profitable trade with the Indians and to extend settlement westward, they became increasingly conscious of the value of the Ohio country, which lay—so to speak—at their back doors. At the same time, the French, holding both Canada and Louisiana, began to realize the importance of the Ohio as a means of communication between their American possessions. Their infant colony in the Illinois country, which they hoped to make the granary of New France, would be threatened, too, if the British advanced west of the mountains.

The value of the Ohio as a link between Canada and Louisiana was emphasized in 1739 when an expedition headed by the Baron de Longueuil[2] traveled by way of Lake Chautauqua, Conewango Creek, the Allegheny River, and the Ohio, to join other forces from Michilimackinac, Detroit, the Illinois, and Louisiana in a campaign against the Chickasaw Indians in northern Mississippi. Here was a striking demonstration of the importance of the Ohio to the French empire in North America. Here also was an opportunity to acquire knowledge of the region in preparation for future operations there. The young engineer, Chaussegros de Léry,[3] gathered data for the first reasonably accurate map of the Ohio country, and many of the officers

---

[1] Marcel Trudel, "L'affaire Jumonville," *Revue d'Histoire de l'Amérique Française,* Vol. VI, p. 340.

[2] Charles Le Moyne, second Baron de Longueuil, born in 1687, was a member of an outstanding colonial family, which from humble beginnings had risen to wealth and nobility in Canada. Among his father's brothers were Iberville and Bienville. According to M. H. Long, *A History of the Canadian People,* I, 145, "Of all the titles of honour bestowed by the French Crown on the seigneurs of the old régime only that of Baron de Longueuil retains legal recognition to the present day."

[3] Joseph Gaspard Chaussegros de Léry (1721-1797) was the son of the chief engineer of Quebec. He was to serve under Marin and Contrecoeur in the Ohio campaigns from 1753 to 1755. His Journal for 1754-1755, covering part of those campaigns, was translated and published by the Pennsylvania Historical Commission in 1940.

3

and cadets serving under Longueuil in 1739 took part in the later Ohio campaigns.[4]

The real French claim then was based on natural boundaries and ease of communication, and the claim that La Salle had discovered the Ohio was essentially only an argument for diplomats to use, for no one brought that up until the other factors came to the fore. The French maintained that the Ohio was the normal and natural communication between Canada and Louisiana, and that the natural barrier of the Appalachians separated the British colonies from the Ohio.

The British colonies of Pennsylvania and Virginia had claims to the Ohio region which were equally valid from their point of view. Both regarded the Ohio country as a natural avenue for expansion, as a contiguous area. Both had charters from the King covering part or all of the region, depending on future boundary determinations. Both had sent out agents and traders to deal with the Indians there, and had developed treaty relationships with various tribes. And high diplomacy, as early as 1713, gave a degree of justification to the British claim, for France conceded in the fifteenth article of the Treaty of Utrecht that the Iroquois were subjects of Great Britain, "quinque nationes, sive cantones Indorum, Magnae Britanniae imperio subjectas."[5] Since the other tribes of the Ohio valley were under the protection of the Iroquois Long House, the British regarded this clause as a recognition of their claim.

In point of actual fact, there were British traders and trading posts in the Ohio country before the French began to take steps to seize it. As early as 1726, the French Company of the Indies expressed concern because some Englishmen had "already made an establishment on the upper part of the Ohio River," and urged that a French

---

[4] Among them were Legardeur de Saint-Pierre, Coulon de Villiers, two of the Joncaires, Repentigny, Benoist, Ligneris, and Portneuf.

[5] Treaty of Utrecht, 1713, printed in the Latin original and in French in *Mémoires des Commissaires du Roi et de Ceux de Sa Majesté Britannique Sur les Possessions et les Droits Respectifs des Deux Couronnes en Amérique* (Paris, 1755), Tome II, 113 and following. Article XV is on pages 129-130. The French argued that this applied only to the persons of the Iroquois, and besides, that "no Englishman would dare, without running the risk of being murdered, to tell the Iroquois they were British subjects." Theodore Calvin Pease, ed., *Anglo-French Boundary Disputes in the West, 1749-1763* (Collections of the Illinois State Historial Library, Volume XXVII), 222-224. Still, the French had recognized them as British subjects.

post be established as a counter-measure.[6] By the middle of the century, a summary in the Provincial Papers of Pennsylvania could report,

> Croghan and others had Stores on the Lake Erie . . . up and down all that fine country watered by the branches of the Miamis, Scioto, and Muskingum Rivers, and upon the Ohio from Bockaloons an Indian town near its head to below the Mouth of the Miami River an extent of 500 miles on one of the most beautiful Rivers in the world . . .[7]

Marquis de La Galissonnière.
—from Parkman, "Montcalm and Wolfe."

With this activity of the traders there was combined the not unsuccessful effort of the Pennsylvania and Virginia governments to win the friendship and alliance of the Indians of the Ohio, while companies were formed to promote settlement and carry on trade west of the Alleghenies. In 1744, by the Treaty of Lancaster, the British obtained half a million acres west of the mountains from the Indians; this was the basis for the formation of the Ohio Company. The French could plainly see that, unless this region were to fall to the British by default, they had to act.

[6] Pierre Margry, ed., *Découvertes et établissements des Français.* . . . (Paris, 1888), VI, 658-660.

[7] Provincial Papers, XIII, 9-13, printed in *Wilderness Chronicles,* 29-36.

The Marquis de La Galissonnière,[8] the distinguished naval officer who became Governor of New France in 1747, was quick to see the significance of the Ohio as a link between Canada and Louisiana, and to take action to strengthen the French claim to it. First, he disposed of the British claim through the Iroquois. In November, 1748, he held a council at Montreal with deputies from five of the Six Nations of the Iroquois, all but the Mohawks, and told them how the British now considered them "vassals," who were "bound to go to war for the English," whenever they were ordered. The Indian spokesmen, as might have been expected, denied this heatedly—"the Six Iroquois Nations were not subjects of England," and "they had not ceded to anyone their lands, which they hold only of Heaven."[9] With that taken care of, his next step was to send out an expedition to take formal possession of the region, and to impress the Indians with French power. This was Céloron's expedition of 1749.

"With a detachment composed of one Captain, eight subaltern officers, six Cadets, one Chaplain, twenty soldiers, one hundred and eighty Canadians, and about thirty Indians,"[10] Céloron de Blainville[11] left La Chine at the head of the rapids of the St. Lawrence above Montreal, on June 15, 1749. By July 6 he had reached Fort Niagara, and the next day men, supplies, and canoes began to move over the Niagara portage to Lake Erie, under the direction of Contrecoeur, his second in command. This task was completed by the 14th, and the ex-

[8] Roland Michel Barrin, Marquis de La Galissonnière (1693-1756), had declined appointment as Governor in 1747, but after the Marquis de la Jonquière was captured by the English, he took La Jonquière's place until he was released. La Galissonnière was a very able and aggressive executive. His reports on Canada's resources and their potential development, and on the ways in which British power in America might be checked and confined, were the most significant results of his brief administration. When he returned to France in the fall of 1749, he was appointed one of the French members of the joint commission to consider the disputed colonial boundaries. After the Seven Years' War broke out, he commanded the Mediterranean squadron which defeated the unfortunate British Admiral Byng in April, 1756.

[9] Conference between M. de la Galissonnière and the Iroquois, November 2, 1748, in E. B. O'Callaghan, ed., *Documents Relative to the Colonial History of the State of New York*, X, 186-188.

[10] "Céloron's Journal," in C. B. Galbreath, ed., *Expedition of Céloron to the Ohio Country in 1749*, 13.

[11] Pierre Joseph Céloron de Blainville (1693-1759) became an ensign in 1715, a lieutenant in 1731, and a captain in 1738. He commanded at Detroit from 1742 to 1744, at Niagara in 1744 and 1745, and at Fort St. Frederic in 1747. After his famous expedition, he again commanded at Detroit, and in 1755 became a major at Montreal. Incorrectly, he is sometimes called Céloron de Bienville, perhaps by confusion with the famous Bienville of Louisiana.

pedition set out on Lake Erie, headed for the Chautauqua portage. Delayed by a storm, it was not until July 16 that they reached the landing place at Chatakoin,[12] where the second portage began. It took Céloron's detachment a month and a day to come from Montreal to the beginning of the portage into the Ohio country.

By July 22 the men had carried the canoes and supplies over the portage to the head of Lake Chautauqua, and on the 23rd they voyaged down the lake to its outlet, which they entered on the 24th. At noon on the 29th of July, the expedition completed its descent of Conewango Creek and entered the Belle Rivière—that is, the Allegheny River at Warren. To the French, as to the Indians, the Allegheny River was the upper part of the Belle Rivière or Ohio.

Here a main purpose of the expedition became evident. On the south bank of the Allegheny, opposite the mouth of the Conewango, Céloron had a lead plate buried whose inscription gave notice "of the renewal of possession which we have taken of the said river Ohio, and of all those which fall into it, and of all the territories on both sides as far as the source of the said rivers."[13] He also fastened to a tree a sheet metal sign with the French King's coat of arms. By these ceremonies at what is now Warren, Pennsylvania, on July 29, 1749, the Ohio country was declared a possession of Louis XV. Actual occupation of the country to enforce this declaration would be necessary to make it effective, but nominally it marked the beginning of the dispute over the Ohio.

The next day, at the village of Kachinodiagon,[14] where Brokenstraw Creek enters the Allegheny, Céloron held a council with the Indians, carrying out another objective of his expedition. He told the Indians about the evil intentions of the English, who wanted to steal their

[12] A French form of Chautauqua, used to designate this point on Lake Erie, now Barcelona Harbor, north of Westfield, New York.

[13] "Céloron's Journal," loc. cit., 18. Apparently, this lead plate did not stay in the ground long, but was dug up by the Indians, who delivered it to William Johnson on December 4, 1750. However, there is a discrepancy between the text of the inscription as given in Céloron's Journal and that on the plate given to Johnson. The first says that the plate was buried at the junction of the Ohio and the Conewango; and the second that it was buried at the junction of the Ohio and the Tchadakoin—i.e., the outlet of Chautauqua Lake. Of course, these two streams do not join, for the outlet is a tributary of the Conewango. It may be that when this error was discovered, the plate was discarded, or that the Indians actually stole it, as they told Johnson.

[14] The French called it Paille Coupée (Cut Straw), and the English called it Buckaloons, a corruption of a Delaware name. The site is near Irvine, nine miles down the Allegheny from Warren.

7

One of Céloron's Lead Plates. Found at the mouth of the Great Kanawha River in 1846, and now in the possession of the Virginia Historical Society.

—from Severance, *"An Old Frontier of France,"* courtesy of Buffalo Historical Society.

land, he said; and he warned them against dealing or trading with the English. He urged them to send any English traders home, promising to send out French traders to replace them. To this the Indians appeared to agree, although it is difficult to believe that they did expel the English traders, considering the serious plight to which they were reduced in the winter of 1753-54 when the English really were driven away.

Similar ceremonies and Indian councils took place elsewhere on Céloron's journey down the river. At Venango, the Indian village and trading post at the mouth of the Rivière aux Boeufs (French Creek), the English trader and the blacksmith, with most of the Indians, fled into the woods, and the five or six Iroquois who remained were not very friendly. Céloron warned them, too, about the evil intentions of the English, but seems not to have found his audience appreciative, for he went on his way immediately. He did not bury a lead plate at the mouth of French Creek, as might have been expected, but nine miles farther down "near an immense stone upon which certain figures are rudely enough carved."[15] This is now known as Indian God Rock.

The voyage continued to Attiqué, whose inhabitants had fled; to the old abandoned Shawnee village of Chartier's Town, where the French encountered six English traders and warned them not to come to the Ohio again; to the village at the Rocher Ecrite or Written Rock (McKee's Rocks) from which Queen Allaquippa and her people had withdrawn. Here they met more English traders and gave them the usual warning. Finally, on August 8, Céloron's detachment came to Chiningué or Logstown, a multiple village of Iroquois, Shawnees, Delawares, and other Indians, which was the great trading center of the Ohio. This was about eighteen miles below present-day Pittsburgh, and near the location of modern Ambridge.

Céloron spent three days at Chiningué, in council with the various Indian tribes, taking extra precautions for the safety of his force in a decidedly uneasy situation. The Indians heard the French warnings and admonitions respectfully, and returned agreeable answers. But Céloron doubted their sincerity, and wrote: ". . . There is little reliance to be placed in the promise of such people, and the more so, . . . since their personal interests make them look with favorable eyes on the English, who give them their merchandise at one-fourth the price." The only way to win them over, he thought, would be "by furnishing them merchandise at the same price as the English; the difficulty is to find out the means."[16] He summoned before him the

---

[15] "Céloron's Journal," *loc. cit.*, 26.
[16] "Céloron's Journal," *loc. cit.*, 34-35.

leaders of the English traders, and warned them to leave the Ohio country, which they promised to do, doubtless with tongue in cheek. Thus he went through all the motions and repeated all the words designed to establish French possession of the Ohio, and continued on his way down river, knowing that the effect was gone virtually as soon as he was.

The expedition descended the Ohio as far as the Miami River, where it turned northward, finally reaching Detroit early in October. Along the way, more lead plates were buried, and at the Indian villages on their route, Scioto and Pickawillany, he held councils with the Indians, much like the earlier sessions. But even his chaplain, Father Bonnecamps, remarked that the Ohio region was "little known to the French, and, unfortunately, too well known to the English," that the latter were "already far within our territory; and, what is worse, they are under the protection of a crowd of Indians whom they entice to themselves."[17] Céloron himself realized that his expedition by itself would have no lasting results, for he observed at the end of his journal: "All that I can say is, that the nations of these localities are very badly disposed towards the French, and are entirely devoted to the English. I do not know in what way they could be brought back."[18]

Even before Céloron's return, La Galissonnière told his successor the Marquis de la Jonquière, that "for something permanent, we must establish one or more trading posts on the Belle Rivière or in its vicinity, and especially toward its headwaters." La Jonquière thought that "these posts might have the inconvenience of making contraband trade easier," but La Galissonnière argued that "this ought to be risked, because without it the English would undoubtedly locate there, and through this would be in a position to pentrate to all our trading posts and cut the communication with Louisiana."[19]

In 1750, Philippe Thomas de Joncaire[20] was sent to the Belle Rivière, to establish a trading post at Chiningué or Logstown, and in the next two years a number of French traders were officially licensed to trade there. Louis Boucher de Niverville, Sieur de

[17] "Journal of Father Bonnecamps," in Galbreath, *loc. cit.,* 90.

[18] "Céloron's Journal," *loc. cit.,* 57.

[19] La Jonquière to the Minister, September 20, 1749, in *Wilderness Chronicles,* 26-27.

[20] Born in 1707, the eldest son of Louis Thomas and Magdelene (Le Guay) de Joncaire. He and his younger brother Chabert inherited their father's influence and prestige among the Iroquois and especially among the Senecas. Joncaire is sometimes said to have had an Indian mother, but this must refer only to his adoption, and may also reflect his complete adaptation to Indian life.

10

Montisambert, and Philippe Dagneau, Sieur de la Saussaye, both hired men in 1751 and 1752 to go with them to "Chinainguay" and elsewhere on the Belle Rivière. Other Ohio traders were Gaspard Normand, Joseph Provenché, and Jacques Marie Nolan Lamarque.[21] Some of these Frenchmen must have been on the Ohio before, but now they came with the official blessing of the Governors of New France.

Marquis Duquesne.
—Public Archives of Canada.

The final step of sending a strong French force to the Ohio region, and of building and garrisoning forts at key points, was delayed until the Marquis Duquesne became Governor in the summer of 1752. Governor de la Jonquière had died before he could do more than encourage traders to go to the Belle Rivière. Troubles with the Indians in the vicinity of the Miami River, and trading and exploring ventures farther west, absorbed his attention. His successor as acting Governor, the Canadian-born Baron de Longueuil, pleaded the "insufficiency of

[21] "Répertoire des engagements pour l'ouest conservés dans les Archives Judiciaires de Montréal," in *Rapport de l'archiviste de la province de Québec* [hereafter, RAPQ] (1930-1931), 353-453. These indentures or contracts of the men hired by the traders include only those made and recorded at Montreal; there may be others recorded at Quebec and Three Rivers.

11

provisions, canoes, and time," and seemed to think that reinforcement of Detroit and its outlying posts would meet the situation.[22] It was later charged that Longueuil was opposed to any military action on the Belle Rivière. Bigot said that he wanted "to leave the Belle Rivière at peace, having a special respect and consideration for the Iroquois who dwell there." When the Intendant protested, "the Governor answered sharply that the English were trading there before us; that it was not just to chase them out; that at most the river belonged to the Iroquois; and that we had only to supply their needs, as the English were doing, for these last to withdraw of their own accord, when they saw they could not earn a living there."[23]

Later, Duquesne explained his failure to employ any of the Longueuil family on the Belle Rivière campaign, by saying that he knew them "to be completely opposed to this undertaking . . ."[24] It would therefore appear that the leading French Canadian in high office, and the people around him, French colonials as opposed to officials from France itself, did not favor aggressive action on the Ohio River. Wishing to get along with their neighbors and to avoid war, they were more interested in developing the colony and extending the fur trade than in any imperial ventures. The French Canadians would have to bear the burden and suffer the consequences of a policy they did not favor.

---

[22] Longueuil to Rouillé, April 21, 1752, in O'Callaghan, ed., *Documents Relative to the Colonial History of the State of New York*, X, 245-251.

[23] Bigot to the Minister, October 26, 1752, *Wilderness Chronicles*, 40. Of course, Bigot wanted to put Longueuil in a bad light, but there is little reason to think that he misrepresented Longueuil's attitude. Oddly enough, Bigot came to a similar conclusion after the event, writing in 1754 "that, after full reflection, it would have perhaps been better to be satisfied with passing along the Belle Rivière and seizing the English traders, without establishing posts there and without making the great stir there which the expedition produced." Guy Frégault, *François Bigot, Administrateur français*, 72.

[24] Duquesne to the Minister, October 31, 1753, *Wilderness Chronicles*, 55-58.

NEW FRANCE PLANS AN EXPEDITION

Ange de Menneville, Marquis Duquesne, who arrived at Quebec on July 30, 1752, and took over the government from the Baron de Longueuil, was a lordly and even arrogant man, stubborn and self-important, who could be expected to pursue a strong and aggressive policy. He may have owed his appointment to the influence of the Marquis de La Galissonnière; and he resumed the former Governor's policy of extending French rule into the Ohio country. His was a famous name, for his great-uncle Abraham Duquesne, the first Marquis, had been a naval hero of the reign of Louis XIV.

But the Governor was not the only factor to be reckoned with in Canadian affairs, for the government of New France had two heads. Beside the Governor, who was military commander and personal representative of the King, there was another great officer, the Intendant, who was in charge of justice, police, finance, taxes, and the procurement of supplies. The functions of the Governor and the Intendant overlapped in a bewildering way, so that each was a check on the other.

The Intendant, François Bigot, was a major figure, ranking in historical importance with any of the five men who served as governors during his term of office. Born at Bordeaux in 1703, he was appointed Intendant of New France in 1748. He was an exceptionally able man, but—unfortunately for New France—his great abilities were used primarily to enrich himself and his cronies. It was not at all uncommon in New France for officials to use public office for private gain, but Bigot with his "extensive opportunities and exceptional ingenuity and organizing ability" developed casual practice into "a widespread system for fraud and peculation."[1] Clever and persuasive, combining the arts of a promoter and a courtier, he quickly fell in with the new Governor's plans for the Ohio expedition, possibly scenting fresh opportunities for jobs for his friends, for making profits in the purchase of supplies, and for stifling some of the discontent his stringent taxes and levies had aroused.

The expedition to the Belle Rivière, as the French called the Ohio and the country which it watered, was to involve a great deal of expense. A force of more than two thousand men was to be sent there to build several forts at strategic points, and to establish French

---

[1] Adam Shortt, ed., *Documents Relating to Canadian Currency, Exchange and Finance During the French Period*, II, 767, note.

control over the region by overawing its Indian inhabitants. Bigot outlined the plans in his letter to the Minister on October 26, 1752:

> To accomplish this, it is necessary to send 2000 Frenchmen with 200 of our domiciliated Indians to this river by way of the Chatakoui portage in the spring; to build a store house at the lower end of this portage on the shore of Lake Erie, and another at the end of this same portage on Lake Chatakoüin; likewise, to make a fort at La Paille Coupée where M. de Joncaire is located, another at the Written Rock or at Chiningué, and a third at Sonhioto. The garrisons of these forts will be taken from the 2000 men; the remainder will go to spend the winter with the Illinois, if they see they will be unable to reach Montreal in the fall, which seemingly will not be possible, since the 200 men who made this same journey 3 years ago, and who had no fort to build, had great difficulty reaching Montreal in the first days of November.[2]

The Intendant set to work gathering supplies for this major venture. This was anything but a simple task, for even in ordinary times the produce of New France barely sufficed for her needs. That year the crops had been very poor in Canada, and there was a serious shortage of food. Bigot actually had to buy flour and corn in New England to supply this expedition to western Pennsylvania.

For command of the expedition Governor Duquesne selected Pierre Paul de la Malgue, Sieur de Marin, a tough old veteran of sixty years, who had been commander of the Fort de la Baie des Puants, on Green Bay in Lake Michigan. There he had carried on the fur trade in a monopoly of which the profits were shared by Governor de la Jonquière and the Intendant Bigot. His personal reputation was not of the best. At the time he was made a captain in 1748, La Galissonnière excused his faults to the minister, "It is his own personal misfortune if he has in his heart some of the low principles which are attributed to him; that would not prevent making use of him with precaution. There are very few perfect men, and the service is full of very useful men who are very bad at heart."[3] La Galissonnière may have meant that he lacked the polish and good manners of the officers from France, and that he had a very bad temper, for Duquesne in eulogizing him after his death mentioned his "half-ferocious disposition."[4] His letters give the impression of a serious and plain man, with a strong sense of duty. For this assignment he seemed well adapted. As Bigot wrote, Marin was chosen "for his reputation as the most feared and respected

---

[2] Bigot to the Minister, October 26, 1752, in *Wilderness Chronicles*, 39-43.

[3] La Galissonnière to Maurepas, October 12, 1748, quoted in Frégault, *Bigot*, I, 366.

[4] Duquesne to the Minister, November 2, 1753, *Wilderness Chronicles*, 59.

by the Indian tribes, and for having the most experience and authority."[5]

Duquesne gratified Bigot by naming Michel Jean Hugues Péan as the second in command. Péan was said to be the wealthiest man in Canada, and a long-time associate of the Intendant in his various business dealings. His wife, Angélique des Méloizes, was a brilliant and attractive woman, who had no scruples about charming the heads of New France for the advancement of her husband and their families. Even though the Intendant wrote that Péan was "the most capable officer that he had in the colony,"[6] and the Governor found him "endowed with a great deal of capacity, intelligence, and executive ability,"[7] this appointment made tongues wag in Quebec. Born in 1723, he was only thirty years old when the Belle Rivière campaign began.

Another of the chief officers was the Chevalier François Le Mercier, who was in charge of engineering and artillery, and entrusted with the care and distribution of munitions. A cousin of Péan, he was born in France in 1722, and came to Canada in 1739 or 1740 as a recruit. Showing aptitude for the military profession, he was sent to France for special study of engineering and artillery methods. After his return to Canada in the spring of 1750, he gained promotion, first as lieutenant, and then as captain, of a company of gunners. It was Le Mercier who designed and built the French forts in western Pennsylvania.

Not less important to the success of the expedition was the commander of Fort Niagara, Claude Pierre Pécaudy de Contrecoeur. Born in 1706, Contrecoeur had been Céloron's second-in-command on the expedition of 1749, and was placed in command of the fort at the mouth of the Niagara River in the summer of 1752. Péan was his nephew, his sister's son, and Le Mercier was also a relative. All the men, all the supplies, all the equipment for the new forts, had to reach their destination by way of Fort Niagara and the Niagara portage road, and the commander there was a key figure in the Ohio campaigns from the very beginning.

Both Marin and Péan had been involved with the Intendant Bigot in various financial deals. Bigot and Marin had shared in the profits from the fur trade at the post of La Baie where Marin had commanded,

[5] Bigot to the Minister, October 26, 1752, *Wilderness Chronicles,* 42.

[6] Bigot to the Minister, October 26, 1752, *Wilderness Chronicles,* 42.

[7] Duquesne to Contrecoeur, May 22, 1753, Archives du Séminaire de Québec, V-V, 1:17.

and Péan was even more closely involved in Bigot's monopolies and speculations. Now the purchase, gathering, and transportation of supplies provided a golden opportunity for graft, of which Bigot and Péan at least seem to have taken fullest advantage.[8] Even of Duquesne himself it has been said that he "did not disdain a deal."[9] Le Mercier

Michel-Jean-Hugues Péan
—from "Rapport de l'archiviste de la
province de Québec pour 1928-1929."

accumulated great wealth during his service in Canada. Perhaps fortunately for their reputations, Marin died and Duquesne retired as governor long before the economic collapse of New France compelled an investigation. After the war was over, Bigot, Péan, Le Mercier, and some of their associates landed in jail, and were brought

[8] Marin may have disappointed Bigot's expectations, for he actually embarrassed the Intendant's underlings by investigation of shortages in the weight of provisions.

[9] Frégault, *Bigot,* II, 68.

to trial.[10] At the very least, it can be said that business and family ties outweighed military considerations in selecting the leaders of the expedition to the Belle Rivière.

While the Governor and the Intendant were making their preparations at Quebec and Montreal, Contrecoeur at Niagara received orders to hurry the completion of the new portage road from Fort Niagara at the mouth of the Niagara River to Little Fort Niagara, the post of Joncaire de Chabert, above the falls. Carpenters and sawyers were

Madame Péan, née Angélique des Méloizes
—from "Rapport de l'archiviste de la province de Quebec pour 1928-1929."

sent him to begin the building of boats. Provision for transportation was a necessary first step in the preparations for the campaign, and this must have given the Niagara commander his first inkling that an expedition was planned.

[10] Bigot was found guilty and stripped of his entire fortune; Péan had to disgorge 600,000 livres; Le Mercier was cleared.

17

His first definite information reached him late in the fall of 1752. On October 5, the Governor wrote him "in the greatest secrecy" that the following spring two thousand men would be coming his way "to reestablish a communication which we would soon lose without this step."[11] On October 18, Duquesne wrote "in strict confidence" to give more details: "In the course of the month of May I shall send from Montreal 300 soldiers, 1700 *habitants,* and about 200 Indians whom I am assigning to go and seize and establish themselves on the Belle Riviere, which we are on the verge of losing if I do not make this hasty but indispensable effort."[12]

In the same letter, the Governor announced his intention of sending an advance party to Chatakoin, the Lake Erie terminus of the Chautauqua portage which had been used by the expeditions of Longueuil and Céloron. In January he would send ahead "about 400 men, almost all workmen," who were to be employed "in the construction necessary for the portage of Chatakoin, in order to shelter from the ravages of the weather the military equipment and food supplies" which were to be sent there.[13] The original intention was that Marin's expedition should reach the Allegheny River by way of the Chautauqua route.

Contrecoeur was to build many boats and pirogues for the expedition, and also to construct warehouses to protect the supplies on the way. As a measure of how much would be needed, the Governor again, on November 14, emphasized the size of the projected campaign: "You know the extent of my project which involves the following: 2200 men to transport; four forts to construct and all the paraphernalia which is involved in such an operation; provisions for a year."[14] The levy of the *habitants* to serve as militia men was already in progress. "Give me your suggestions, please,"[15] wrote the Governor, as he grappled with the many problems involved in this movement of troops and supplies from Montreal to the Belle Rivière.

---

[11] Duquesne to Contrecoeur, October 5, 1752, *Papiers Contrecoeur,* 14-15.

[12] Duquesne to Contrecoeur, October 18, 1752, *Papiers Contrecoeur,* 16-17.

[13] *Ibid.*

[14] Duquesne to Contrecoeur, November 14, 1752, *Papiers Contrecoeur,* 17-19.

[15] *Ibid.*

BOISHEBERT LEADS THE ADVANCE

On the first of February, 1753, the advance party left Montreal under the command of Charles Deschamps de Boishébert, who was to prepare the way for the main expedition under Marin. Although he was only twenty-four years old, he had already been in the service for eleven years, and had just returned from a visit to Paris, carrying dispatches for Governor de la Jonquière. He returned with the new Governor, Marquis Duquesne, and their shipboard acquaintance doubtless led to this important assignment for the young man.[1]

The nature of this assignment was outlined by Varin, Bigot's deputy at Montreal:

> This detachment, which is made up of 250 men, including 20 or 22 carpenters and masons, has orders to work during the stay it will have to make at Niagara, if it arrives there on the 15th or 20th of March, as there is reason to believe. The work will consist of enlarging the portage warehouses and building pirogues; as soon as navigation opens, transporting the detachment in the boats that are being made there, from the Niagara portage to the Tchatacoüen portage, where a fortified storehouse will be built.[2]

The journey to Niagara in February's unpredictable weather was made difficult by ill-timed thaws and floods. According to Boishébert's own statement, "he endured great hardships, and contributed a great deal in the execution of this plan, by his care in preserving the provisions for the place where they were to stay, and by taking most of them from the soldiers' hands, in order to make a storehouse of them on the Bay of Quinté."[3] Apparently, he was to leave supplies there on the north shore of Lake Ontario for the use of later detachments, but it got him into difficulty. "This necessary and required precaution caused him great embarrassment, for he found himself on the road without provisions in the midst of a country inundated by the flooding of the neighboring rivers. The activity and zeal of Sieur

---

[1] His earlier and later career was chiefly in Acadia, and he distinguished himself in the final campaign before the fall of Canada. The founder of the first white establishment at Erie returned to France in 1760, spent fifteen months in the Bastille awaiting trial on charges of graft, but was eventually cleared. Frégault, *Bigot*, II, 8, note.

[2] Varin to Contrecoeur, February 4, 1753, *Papiers Contrecoeur*, 20-21.

[3] *Mémoire pour le Sieur de Boishébert* . . . (Paris, 1763), translated from a transcript in the Public Archives of Canada. This was the brief submitted in his defense at the trial mentioned in note 1.

Charles Deschamps de Boishébert
—*from Parkman, "Montcalm and Wolfe."*

Joncaire-Chabert, who was entrusted with bringing boats and supplies to him, promptly rescued him from this predicament."[4] As a result, Boishébert cannot have reached Fort Niagara before the middle of March.

Governor Duquesne sent Contrecoeur a succession of orders and suggestions about the use of Boishébert's detachment. Even though he wrote on February 1, "I am leaving entirely in your hands the assignment of his detachment," he added that it could build sheds and "at least a hundred pirogues in which I intend to have Sieur de Boishébert and his detachment go to the portage of Chatacoin when navigation opens."[5] Upon receiving Contrecoeur's letter of December 4, 1752, suggesting that it would be "an easy matter to send this detachment by land to Chatacoin," Duquesne agreed if "it could be supplied so as to wait for the first reinforcement."[6] Péan also urged his uncle to "send this detachment to Chatacoin just as soon as it is possible to do it."[7]

The Governor began to worry about possible Indian attacks on this advance force. On March 19, he told Contrecoeur to have "Sieur de Boishebert take all the precautions imaginable when he lands at the Chatacouin portage, the place which I have always considered the most vital to the success of my project, and which I would have seized already if I had to fear making an establishment against their will, as in the case of the entire Belle Riviere." Scouts should be sent out, he said, and the rest of the detachment should "work on the first fort with as much speed as strength."[8]

Four days later, the Governor changed his mind about the route of the expedition, and wrote again to Contrecoeur:

> After my letter was written, Sir, a famous voyageur who has made seven trips on the Belle Riviere and who is said to be a trustworthy man, has pictured for me all the risks he foresaw in the Chatacouin portage. The approach to it, he says, is very, very risky, especially for boats loaded as much as ours will be. They could not be dragged up on shore like a bark canoe when wind and waves are beating high on a shore bordered with rocks, where there are reefs and no shelter. On the map which this voyageur made from memory and gave me, I immediately chose the harbor marked H, which you will notice is thirteen leagues to the west of Chatacouin, formed by a peninsula which makes a secure refuge in all sorts of weather.[9]

---

[4] *Ibid.*

[5] Duquesne to Contrecoeur, February 1, 1753, *Papiers Contrecoeur*, 19-20.

[6] Duquesne to Contrecoeur, February 11, 1753, *Papiers Contrecoeur*, 22.

[7] Péan to Contrecoeur, February 11, 1753, Archives du Séminaire de Québec, V-V, 1:54.

[8] Duquesne to Contrecoeur, March 19, 1753, *Papiers Contrecoeur* 24-26.

[9] Duquesne to Contrecoeur, March 23, 1753, *Papiers Contrecoeur*, 28-31.

Who was this famous voyageur who called attention to the harbor of Presque Isle? It may have been La Saussaye, who is known to have been on the Ohio in 1739, when he led a Shawnee delegation to Montreal; again in 1749, when he showed Céloron the portage around the shallows of the Chautauqua outlet; and in the 1750's when he was licensed to trade on the Belle Rivière. But other traders might fit Duquesne's description just as well; there can be no certain identification. Even the map which the voyageur made, the first map of Erie harbor, has been lost. It is evident that he was Erie's first booster, for Duquesne continued:

> In addition to the safety which such a good post will give us, it is the place, so I have been assured, where there is the best hunting, fishing, fertile land, immense meadows to feed and raise cattle, where Indian corn grows with unequalled abundance so that it need only be sown.
>
> It is true that there are eight leagues of portage, but the convenience of having horses there will make up for this difficulty.
>
> Consequently, I have decided to send an order to Sieur de Boishebert to land at this harbor, and to have the first fort built near the bank on a small elevation marked I, which I have been told is there, and easily recognized because the ground has been burned over.[10]

Therefore, the site of Fort Presque Isle was chosen by Governor Duquesne, looking at a map in Montreal, and not by a French officer on the ground. The Governor continued to expand upon the advantages of his "discovery:"[11]

> I was told also that in this place there are many more resources than at Chatacoin, such as trees suitable for making pirogues and for the lumber we shall need.
>
> Please notice, Sir, *on the map* how much better it is to establish ourselves preferably at this place which gives us an easy entrance to the Belle Riviere and enables us to avoid all the bad passages from the Paille Coupée to the mouth of the Riviere au Boeuf.[12]

The Governor made it clear that Presque Isle was a pretty well known place: "I expect that, in spite of the knowledge which a number of people have about this peninsula which forms the port in question, you will try to find a guide who can lead the detachment safely, and who can bring news from Sieur Boishebert to me."[13]

---

[10] *Ibid.*

[11] In his letter to the Minister, August 20, 1753 (*Wilderness Chronicles*, 49-53), Duquesne spoke of "the harbor of Presqu'isle, on Lake Erie, which I, very fortunately, discovered." He also called it "the finest spot in nature."

[12] Duquesne to Contrecoeur, March 23, 1753, *loc. cit.*

[13] *Ibid.*

But before this letter changing their destination could reach Niagara, Boishébert and his detachment had already landed at Chatakoin about the middle of April. Duquesne later commented appreciatively on "the plan which Sieur de Boishebert sent me of the exploration which he made, in which plan he has given me information beyond what I could have hoped for from anyone who is not Marin."[14] Boishébert's explorations extended to the vicinity of Presque Isle, for Duquesne, in mentioning the possible uses of that harbor, commented: "Let me know, please, if in the place marked on the plan of Sieur de Boishebert as suitable for the building of boats, or in the vicinity, the necessary wood will be found."[15]

In the meantime, Governor Duquesne had changed his mind, and decided that the landing at Presque Isle was too risky to entrust to a twenty-four-year-old. The first detachment of the main expedition had left Montreal on April 15, under the command of the engineer Le Mercier. On May 3, the Governor wrote Contrecoeur:

> I am certain that Sieur Le Mercier has told you that what made me decide to send him off so soon, is to investigate all along the coast the places where we can put into port in case of a squall. He will have told you also that, according to the advice given me, we would find obstacles to landing at Presquisle. I decided to send off M. Marin, so that this landing might take place under an officer of consummate experience and with enough forces to meet those who might oppose it.
>
> I believe indeed that Sieur de Boishebert would have carried out this mission perfectly, but if by some misfortune he had not succeeded, I would have reproached myself for the insufficiency of the forces given him for setting up such establishments. Add to this, too, that this officer is not of suitable rank for my peace of mind in this operation.[16]

In a postscript the Governor sent a consoling message to young Boishébert: "As it is M. Marin who is going to lead the landing, please tell Sieur de Boishebert, whom I have not the time to write, that I am immensely pleased with his conduct . . ."[17]

But the Governor's letter was too late, Contrecoeur had already ordered Boishébert to leave Chatakoin for Presque Isle, and the young officer gained the honor of leading the French landing at Presque Isle, and of beginning the first establishment there. Probably he was already there when the delaying order was written, for Contrecoeur

---

[14] Or, "from anyone who is not a mariner." There is an untranslatable pun here. Duquesne to Contrecoeur, May 13, 1753, Archives du Séminaire de Québec, V-V, 1:16. Duquesne acknowledged a letter of April 25 from Contrecoeur.

[15] *Ibid.*

[16] Duquesne to Contrecoeur, May 3, 1753, *Papiers Contrecoeur*, 36-37.

[17] *Ibid.*

had instructed him to leave for the new location on the first of May. Duquesne accepted the accomplished fact with good grace on May 13:

> As you assure me, Sir, that no obstacle will be found to the landing at the Presquisle, which is demonstrated by your fixing the departure of Sieur de Boishebert for the first of May, I shall have no worry over the fact that he set out with his detachment before the arrival of MM. Marin and Mercier. It cannot but be very advantageous for the speed of the establishments we have to make in that part.
>
> I have no doubt whatever that this commander, who has his share of the vigilance necessary to carry out my plan, will pass very soon to the Presquisle.[18]

The Governor was pleased to hear that the landing was successful, and wrote on June 1 to congratulate Contrecoeur:

> I was delighted to learn that you profited by the fortunate circumstances of tranquility prevailing at the portage of Presqu'isle and sent Sieur de Boishebert there without waiting for M. Marin's arrival. It is to you, Sir, that the King owes the speed which will result from having moved ahead with these establishments, and I shall do my best to make its worth known.[19]

The Governor may have had good intentions about giving credit for this successful opening move of the Ohio campaign, but it never reached the pages of history until the Contrecoeur Papers became available. It has always been thought that Le Mercier discovered Presque Isle, and that Marin was responsible for establishing the fort there, instead of at Chatakoin. How did these errors come about?

Among the soldiers in the advance party was a New Englander named Stephen Coffin, who had been held captive in Quebec ever since the previous war, and had enlisted in the hope of escaping. After he did escape, Coffin made a deposition before William Johnson on January 10, 1754. Until the Contrecoeur Papers came to light, this deposition was the only detailed source on the early stages of the French expedition; this was the source of the errors.

According to Coffin, the detachment was commanded by "Monsr Babeer," a name easily recognized as Boishébert. They set off from Montreal "by Land [and] Ice; for Lake Erie," stopping on the way "at Cadarahqui Fort" and "at Taranto," and remaining at "Niagara

---

[18] Duquesne to Contrecoeur, May 13, 1753, Archives du Séminaire de Québec, V-V, 1:16.

[19] Duquesne to Contrecoeur, June 1, 1753, Archives du Séminaire de Québec, V-V, 1:18. Duquesne acknowledged Contrecoeur's letters of May 7, 8, 17, 18, and 19, but from the order in which matters are discussed in his letter, it may be assumed that Contrecoeur reported the landing's success on May 7 or 8. Allowing a few days for the news to reach Niagara from Presque Isle, the landing there must have taken place about May 3.

Fort 15 days." Then they "sett off by water being April, and Arrived at Chadakoin on Lake Erie, where they were ordered to fell Timber and prepare it for Building a Fort there According to the Governor's Instructions." So far, everything fits with the official letters; now the discrepancies appear:

> . . . but Mr Morang coming up with 500 men, and 20 Indians put a stop to the Erecting of a Fort at that place, by reason of his not Liking the Situation, and the river of Chadakoins being too shallow to cary any Craft with provisions &^c to belle rivere; The Deponent says there Arose a warm debate between Messrs Babeer and Morang thereon, the first Insisting on building a Fort there Agreeable to his Instructions, otherwis on Morangs giving him an Instrument in Writting to satisfy the Governor in that point, which Morang did, and then ordered Monsr Mercie, who was both Commissary and Enginer; to go along said Lake, and Look for a good Situation, which he found and returned in three days, it being 15 Leagues to the S W of Chadakoin; they were then all ordered to repair thither, when they arrived, there were about 20 Indians fishing in the Lake, who Immediatly quit it on Seeing the French . . .[20]

People can be seen fishing at the entrance to Erie harbor almost any time in the spring, but that is the only thing in this account that can be trusted. The Governor himself had ordered the move to Presque Isle, and it is impossible to imagine the young officer disputing his order. Neither Marin nor Le Mercier could have been there; they were still on the way from Montreal when the landing was made at Presque Isle. It was Boishébert who explored the Lake Erie shore and Presque Isle Bay; it was he who made the landing at Presque Isle and began the fort, with his advance party of workmen. It is probable that Coffin had only the haziest notion as to who was who among his officers; and when he made his deposition to Johnson nine months later, his memory of what had happened may have been faulty.

As a result of Coffin's statement, all the existing historical accounts of the coming of the French to Presque Isle give the credit to Marin and Le Mercier for the discovery of Erie harbor and the decision to locate Fort Presque Isle there.

Even Frank H. Severance, in *An Old Frontier of France*,[21] followed the account given by Stephen Coffin, for lack of anything better, though he called the deposition "a dubious English narrative." He

---

[20] Examination of Stephen Coffin, January 10, 1754, Sir William Johnson Manuscripts, Vol. 23, p. 170. New York State Library. Other versions called Deposition of Stephen Coffen, Provincial Record, M, 304-307, printed in *Wilderness Chronicles*, 43-45; *Colonial Records*, VI, 9-10; etc.

[21] Severance, *op. cit.*, II, 5, 21-22, 27-28.

was very close to the truth, however. A few pages later, he actually used Boishébert's statement, as quoted earlier, and he even included Boishébert's final sentence on the campaign of 1753: "They finally reached the Presqu'Isle, the fort was built, a garrison established, and they returned to Quebec."[22] Not connecting Boishébert with Coffin's "Babeer," Severance failed to see that the French source contradicted the English one.

An unnamed voyageur pointed out the Presque Isle on a map to Governor Duquesne. The Governor himself ordered the change in route, and selected the site of the fort. Boishébert made preliminary explorations of the bay, brought his detachment there about the third of May, and began Fort Presque Isle. Of course, he did not finish the fort, for Marin took over the command in June; but it was the twenty-four-year-old Boishébert who began the first white establishment at Erie.

---

[22] *Mémoire pour le Sieur de Boishébert* . . . (Paris, 1763), translated from transcript in the Public Archives of Canada. Severance quoted this passage, *op. cit.*, II, 28.

The Presque Isle in the 1750's. A page from the Journal of Chaussegros de Léry, 1754-1755, showing the peninsula and harbor.

—*Archives du Séminaire de Québec.*

THE FRENCH FORTIFY THE PRESQUE ISLE PORTAGE

Boishébert's detachment of two hundred men had occupied the beachheads at Chatakoin and Presque Isle, but the French position at the gateway to the Belle Rivière would not be really secure until the main army of two thousand men had arrived and forts had been built. This army began leaving Montreal the middle of April in separate detachments, so that the entire troop movement was not completed until summer. The first detachment of seventy men left under Le Mercier on April 16, Marin set out with a large detachment on April 26, and other detachments followed until Péan brought the rear guard and moved the last of the supplies to Presque Isle, during the summer.

This tremendous undertaking represented a huge outlay not only in material resources, but also in human labor and lives. Only a hardy and tough people like the French Canadians could have faced such a wilderness campaign. Duquesne himself later said that "The Canadians are the only people in the world who would be capable of sleeping in the open air, and able to endure the immense labor which this detachment performed in transporting baggage on two portages, one of seven leagues and the other of three leagues."[1] More than two thousand men, with all their equipment and supplies, had to travel over five hundred miles of river and lake and portage road. The back-breaking toil of rowing and paddling, and the weary marching under heavy loads, can scarcely be imagined.

Marin left Montreal on April 26 for La Chine, the embarkation point above the rapids of the St. Lawrence where there were "sheds and storehouses" for the "goods intended for the Upper Country."[2] Here the boats were loaded, the men assigned to them, and the expedition organized for its long journey. Marin departed with his detachment from this jumping-off place on the morning of the 27th, after some difficulty over the desertion of two unwilling conscripts. About this Duquesne wrote him "not to lose patience if you have some annoyances," and promised to make examples of the deserters if they were caught.[3]

Marin's detachment with its equipment and supplies moved up the St. Lawrence to Lake Ontario, reaching Presentation, the French mis-

---

[1] Duquesne to the Minister, November 2, 1753, *Wilderness Chronicles*, 58-60.

[2] Memoir on the State of New France, RAPQ (1923-1924), 53-54.

[3] Duquesne to Marin, April 27, 1753, *Papiers Contrecoeur*, 34-35.

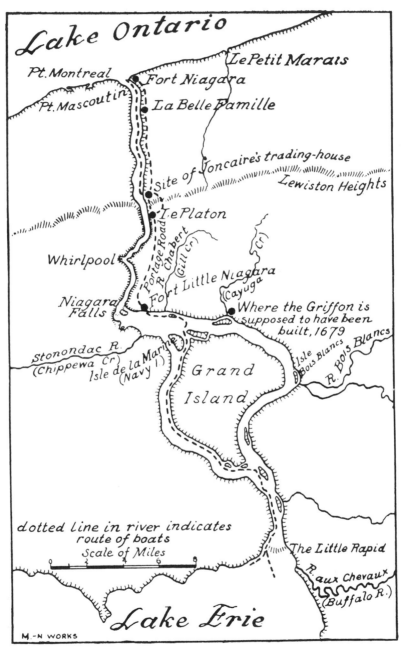

Map of the Niagara Portage.

—from Severance, "An Old Frontier of France,"
courtesy of Buffalo Historical Society.

sionary center, in the first days of May, about the time when Bois-hébert was landing at Presque Isle. From here they rowed and paddled to Fort Frontenac or Cataraqui, where part of the force was transferred to "the three barks of this post to go to Niagara," while the rest continued their journey there "in the bark canoes and bateaux."[4]

Marin and his men reached Fort Niagara at the mouth of the Niagara River by May 19. From here the boats and canoes could go only seven miles up the river before the Niagara gorge brought an end to navigation. Then the baggage, equipment and supplies had to be carried over the portage road up Lewiston Heights and past Niagara Falls to Joncaire de Chabert's post, Little Fort Niagara, where twenty boats and fifty or sixty pirogues were ready for "the passage of the army from Niagara to the portage of the Riviere aux Boeufs."[5]

The portage at Niagara was a confusing and complicated operation, with many problems for Marin, Contrecoeur, and Chabert to solve. Among them were the first recorded labor troubles in the area. The Indians of the locality had customarily been hired to carry goods over the portage on the King's service or for traders. Now they objected to part of the work being done by the soldiers and by teams of horses, and had to be quieted by explanations that this was only to meet an emergency. Marin's soldiers also demanded to be paid for carrying as the Indians were, and to avoid delay he agreed. The Governor told him never to do it again: "You could be reproached for not having enough control to have things done as they have been done since Canada was Canada."[6]

The theft of supplies by the Indians and soldiers conveying them could be prevented only by the most careful supervision, and perishable goods like flour had to be protected from the weather. The very order in which supplies were sent sometimes created difficulties, as when provisions still needed at the lower end were sent to the upper end of the portage. On May 24, Marin wrote "from the Portage," where he was supervising the work, presumably at the foot of Lewiston Heights:

> After your departure from this place, I learned that [the crews of] my 15 canoes had all been lacking salt pork for more than three days. Consequently, they have not had any soup at all and are not

---

[4] Bigot to the Minister, October 26, 1752, *Wilderness Chronicles,* 39-43.

[5] Varin to Contrecoeur, May 10, 1753, Archives du Séminaire de Québec, V-V, 4:300.

[6] Duquesne to Marin, June 13, 1753, Archives du Séminaire de Québec, V-V, 5:62:5.

in shape to work for that reason; that is why I beg you to supply them with some provisions, although none at all are due them. I want only some salt pork; I am sending you a man by canoe . . .[7]

On May 26, he reported progress with the portage:

You can send the two loaded boats as soon as you please, as I have had everything sent up, and nothing more remains here. I am sending you men to get them and transport them immediately so that they will reach me as promptly as possible at the Presquisle. . . . I am very much obliged to you, Sir, for what you have sent me to make soup with, and I can assure you it will be good. All these gentlemen will enjoy it with me.[8]

The liking of Canadians for soup is obviously not of recent origin.

Duquesne was very much pleased to hear of Marin's arrival at Fort Niagara. He wrote that he was sending off reinforcements every day, "more than sufficient for M. Marin to march to the Belle Riviere as soon as the forts are built."[9] The promising outlook led him to express a pious thought:

It seems that up to the present God is favoring the zeal with which I am working for the good of this colony, which the King would be forced to abandon if we lost the communication through the Upper Country. Every moment of the day I pray that He may deign to favor my good intentions.[10]

By the last day of May, Marin was ready to leave the Niagara portage. He sent a quantity of baggage ahead in seventeen boats and thirty-one pirogues, and on the first of June he set out on Lake Erie with sixteen canoe-loads of men. If the weather was favorable, he must have reached the harbor of Presque Isle and the new fort on June 2 or 3. Of course, there were busy days after he landed, and he did not find time to write to Contrecoeur until June 8, when he said, "Upon my arrival at this fort, I found the works making very good progress, and very much in order. You will not be surprised at this, I think, for you know the energy and care manifested by M. Le Mercier."[11]

Le Mercier and his seventy men had reached Presque Isle two or three weeks earlier, for they left Montreal ten days before Marin and a smaller detachment could travel more rapidly. Late in May, Le Mercier had sent "a brief sketch of his works" to Contrecoeur, who forwarded it to the Governor on May 31. Duquesne thought this was

[7] Marin to Contrecoeur, May 24, 1753, Archives du Séminaire de Québec, V-V, 1:60.

[8] Marin to Contrecoeur, May 26, 1753, Archives du Séminaire de Québec, V-V, 1:61.

[9] Duquesne to Contrecoeur, June 1, 1753, Archives du Séminaire de Québec, V-V, 1:18.

[10] Ibid.

[11] Marin to Contrecoeur, June 8, 1753, Archives du Séminaire de Québec, V-V, 1:62.

"more than in proportion to the fewness of the men he has," and asked Marin to "convey to him my satisfaction, and congratulate him for me that your arrival is going to make the works move in accordance with his wishes and his zeal."[12]

Unfortunately, Le Mercier's sketch has been lost, but a later French account described it as a "square fort of squared timbers,"[13] and Duquesne alluded to it as "built piece upon piece."[14] This supporting evidence corroborates Stephen Coffin, who related that Fort Presque Isle was "a square Fort of Chesnut Loggs squared & lapt over each other, to the hight of 15 foot, it is about 120 feet square, [a Log House in each Square, a Gate to the Southward and] another to the Northward [, not one Port Hole] cut in any part of it."[15]

French Fort Presque Isle stood on a little elevation west of the mouth of Mill Creek, overlooking what was then the entrance to the bay. When the Americans came in 1795, they built their fort on the corresponding hill east of Mill Creek to command the bay entrance. The place where the French fort stood was cut away by a brickyard in the nineteenth century, so that our only clue today to the way it overlooked the waters of Presque Isle Bay is the little elevation occupied by the Anthony Wayne Blockhouse.

In June Duquesne heard from Marin that "his whole army is going better and better, and with gaiety in all the work in which it is employed," and observed that it was "a fine prospect for a commander to march at the head of a troop like that."[16] On July 10, Duquesne told Contrecoeur that

All the news which comes to me from the Upper Country assures me that the bands of the Belle Riviere are returning to their village, and not a single Englishman remains there. I am not in the least worried about the success of M. Marin, but I am a great deal concerned about the exorbitant expense of the portages which will certainly go much higher than I had estimated.[17]

[12] Duquesne to Marin, June 13, 1753, Archives du Séminaire de Québec, V-V, 5:62:5.

[13] Memoir on the State of New France, RAPQ (1923-1924), 48.

[14] Duquesne to Marin, July 22, 1753, Archives du Séminaire de Québec, V-V, 5:62:8.

[15] Examination of Stephen Coffin, January 10, 1754, Sir William Johnson Manuscripts, Vol. 23, p. 170. New York State Library. The words in brackets are supplied from Deposition of Stephen Coffen, Provincial Record, M, 304-307, printed in Wilderness Chronicles, 43-49.

[16] Duquesne to Contrecoeur, July 1, 1753, Archives du Séminaire de Québec, V-V, 1:21.

[17] Duquesne to Contrecoeur, July 10, 1753, Archives du Séminaire de Québec, V-V, 1:23.

The same day, the Governor wrote to Marin, noting from his letter of June 20 .

> that you have been relieved of the fear you had lest the Fort de la Presquisle should be an obstacle to the speed of my project; and I have seen also with admiration in the enumeration you give me of the idle men and of those you are keeping busy in so many different jobs, that the impossible is being attempted.
>
> It is, however, not without worry that I see so much work done by so few men, and I am still afraid that they may be overworked, and that the best men may be lacking when they are needed.[18]

While the work on Fort Presque Isle was progressing, Marin turned his attention to the next steps, the improvement of the portage to a stream flowing into the Ohio River system, and the building of a second fort at the southern end of this portage. Sometime in June, he sent two of his officers to look over the portage route and to pick a site for the fort. But he went himself before making a decision. In his letter of July 10, the Governor commented:

> Although I think Sieurs Dubreuil and La Chavignerie are capable of wisely determining the site where the second fort could be located, I have seen with pleasure from the particulars you give me of your journey that you have done better than they did, both as to firewood for the garrison, and also as to the lands suitable for sowing what you consider best for the wellbeing of the garrison.[19]

The site which Marin chose was a knoll on the south bank of Le Boeuf Creek, a short distance above Lake Le Boeuf. Washington later described it as "almost surrounded by the Creek, and a small Branch of it which forms a Kind of Island."[20] Time and the leveling and filling of ground in the growth of the borough of Waterford has changed the contours so that the island character of this site is no longer apparent.

Marin had also pointed out the need for bridges at some points along the portage road, and for a storehouse at a point halfway between the two forts. Duquesne said he could do whatever he thought best: "As to the bridges about which you are talking for the season of high water, that is up to you, Sir, to whom I leave it to order them from the commanding officers in the forts . . ." "With regard to the building at the storehouse of which you speak, remember, Sir, that I have left you free to do for the good of the job what I could not foresee in my instructions."[21]

---

[18] Duquesne to Marin, July 10, 1753, Archives du Séminaire de Québec, V-V, 5:62:6.

[19] *Ibid.*

[20] John C. Fitzpatrick, ed., *The Diaries of George Washington*, I, 59.

[21] Duquesne to Marin, July 10, 1753, Archives du Séminaire de Québec, V-V, 5:62:6.

The building of Fort Le Boeuf was begun on July 12. The day before, Marin wrote Contrecoeur, "I am going tomorrow to the end of the portage to have ovens and a forge built there, and to erect the stockade."[22] The order of mention is interesting—first, cooking facilities; next, the smithy for shoeing horses and repairing tools; and, finally, measures for defense.

Fort Le Boeuf was somewhat smaller than Fort Presque Isle, and, like the first fort, it was square in shape, with bastions at the corners. But instead of being constructed with squared logs laid lengthwise,

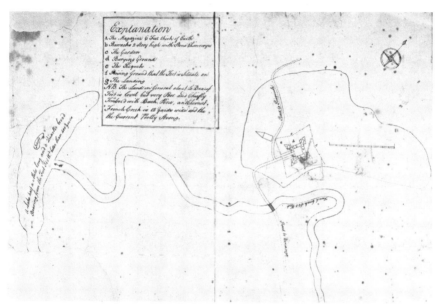

Plan of Fort Le Boeuf made by Thomas Hutchins in 1759.
—*The Historical Society of Pennsylvania.*

it was "a square fort of upright piles."[23] According to Washington's description, in December, 1753,

> Four Houses compose the Sides. The Bastions are made of Piles driven into the Ground, standing more than 12 Feet above it, and sharp at Top: With Port-Holes cut for Cannon, and Loop-Holes for the small Arms to fire through. There are eight 6 *lb*. Pieces mounted, in each Bastion; and one Piece of four Pound before the Gate. In the Bastions are a Guard House, chapel, Doctor's Lodging, and the Commander's private Store; Round which are laid Plat-Forms for the Cannon and Men to stand on.[24]

---

[22] Marin to Contrecoeur, July 11, 1753, Archives du Séminaire de Québec, V-V, 1:64.

[23] Memoir on the State of New France, RAPQ (1923-1924), 48.

[24] Fitzpatrick, ed., *The Diaries of George Washington*, I, 59.

The site of Fort Le Boeuf did not suffer the ignominious fate of the first fort, it was not made into bricks, although the fort itself disappeared with the passing of the French occupation. Other and later historic structures were built there, English and American forts, the Amos Judson House, and the Eagle Hotel. The Amos Judson House and most of the actual area of the French fort now belong to the Commonwealth and are administered by the Pennsylvania Historical and Museum Commission as the Fort Le Boeuf Memorial.

The construction of forts and the building of the portage road were only a part of Marin's complex task. The commander had to see to numerous petty details, even to getting proper feed for the horses and checking into cases of short weight among the provisions.

Horses were needed both to haul timber for the forts and to transport heavy goods over the portage road. By summer there were at least 45 horses at Presque Isle, brought either by contractors or by the army itself.[25] The Indians also brought horses for the French to hire for the portage. Marin therefore had to concern himself with oats and hay for the horses, as well as provisions for the men.

In July Marin became alarmed about shortages in the weight of the barrels of salt pork, and other discrepancies in the provisions. On July 15, he wrote Contrecoeur:

> All the barrels which have come to us, as well as the goods, are in very good condition, but they lack much more than they should of the weight they are supposed to have. I have had a number weighed in my presence, and one after the other they lacked at least seven pounds which was replaced with salt, and that cannot take the place of salt pork in the rations. I told M. Le Mercier to send a report on it to the General, and omit no details. I am advising him also, Sir, that I am asking you in this to please send him a report on the barrels of salt pork which you have both at Niagara and at the little fort, to make mention of everything which is spoiled, and to take about ten by chance from those which seem in good condition and have them weighed, after removing the salt, so that he can see what our subsistence amounts to. Please also have the barrels in poor condition evaluated, so that the storekeeper can have them put in shape when he sends them here. I realize, Sir, the work that is going to give you, but even on this new task depends the success of the King's arms.[26]

---

[25] Two horses sent to Niagara in the fall of 1752, 14 horses taken to Presque Isle by De Langy in June, and 29 horses by St. Blin in July. Varin to Contrecoeur, June 1, 1753, Archives du Séminaire de Québec, V-V, 4:302; Marin to Contrecoeur, July 11, 1753, *loc. cit.*, 1:64.

[26] Marin to Contrecoeur, July 15, 1753, Archives du Séminaire de Québec, V-V, 1:65.

In another letter, Marin remarked,

You have seen the shortages which occur with the salt pork; they are still heavier with the goods, and generally with everything coming to us. Not a package, or at least very few of them, contains what is marked on the invoice. I am having note kept about them as they are opened.[27]

Then Le Mercier, the supply officer, showed Marin orders from a Montreal official, probably Bigot's deputy Varin, who was in charge of the procurement of supplies. According to this, all the storekeepers and clerks were to obey Le Mercier "and not to do or deliver anything but by his orders."[28] Marin wrote a sharp letter of protest:

I think, Sir, that you are not unaware of the fact that all these persons, like everyone else, are subordinate to me, and that if they are not in order, I shall make them so.

*   *   *   *   *

M. le Mercier and I are reporting to the General about the shortages found in the salt pork. We have unpacked for the needs of the service some cases and packages in which errors were found. We shall not fail to keep on checking them every time it is necessary to unpack them.[29]

Varin wrote Contrecoeur that "Marin has a wicked mind which can only presume evil of everyone," and gave a detailed explanation of the discrepancy in the weight of the barrels.[30] He hoped that Marin's second-in-command, Péan, would soon arrive at Presque Isle and put an end to the wrangling.

These and other details took up so much of Marin's time that he forgot to report to the Governor, who wrote a scolding letter on July 22:

It grieves me, Sir, certainly a great deal that, though you know I am keen and impatient, you have already forgotten that I must be unceasingly on the watch to get news from you, and that, since your arrival at Presquisle, I have seen only four of your letters. These, in truth, gave me a great deal of satisfaction, but the long time it has been since I received them is far too long an interval. It makes life so hard for me that I am deciding to send you a messenger by canoe to ask where you are, and what report I am to make to the Minister on the progress of your works, for it would be unheard of if I had to quote to him only the letters which were done on June 27th, which is the date of your last letter.

[27] Letter from Marin, undated. Archives du Séminaire de Québec, V-V, 5:60:11.

[28] Marin to [Varin], July 18, 1753, Archives du Séminaire de Québec, V-V, 5:60:13.

[29] Ibid.

[30] Varin to Contrecoeur, August 18, 1753, Archives du Séminaire de Québec, V-V, 4:311.

The Governor continued, ordering Marin to save time by building Fort Le Boeuf stockade-style, instead of with the logs laid lengthwise as at Fort Presque Isle:

As forts built piece upon piece take more time than those which are made by driving piles four feet into the ground, extending ten or twelve feet above it, you will please conform to this usual way of building them in the Upper Country, according to which I am expecting prompter diligence . . .

Apparently, Varin and other officials who were embarrassed by Marin's investigation of the supplies had misrepresented the situation to the Governor, who concluded with a rather playful warning:

It has been reported to me, but I do not believe a word of it, that you are rejecting all the provisions which had suffered in the Portage of Niagara, without considering that they were exposed to the loss of their quality in the transportation—as if you were within reach of an immense storehouse where freedom of choice was permitted you; and I repeat to you that I do not believe it at all, for it is not at all like you to make such a difficulty, you, Sir, who were born with a hatchet in your hand and with a flour sack for a diaper.[31]

Marin replied to Duquesne on August 3 that Fort Presque Isle had been completed, and that the portage road to Le Boeuf was ready for use. The storehouse halfway along the portage road was ready, and—most important of all—the second fort was well along toward completion at the entrance to the Rivière aux Boeufs. He was having pirogues constructed for the descent to the Ohio, while his men were "actively employed in transporting his stores" over the portage. Even some Indians had come to assist with their horses in the work of the portage.[32]

The Governor related these details to the Minister with great satisfaction on August 20, adding that "There has not been, up to the present time, the least impediment to the considerable movements I have caused to be made." "Everything announces," he said, "the successful execution of my project, unless some unforeseen accident has occured, and the only anxiety I feel is, that the River au Boeuf portage will delay the entrance of our troops into the Beautiful River, as it is long . . ."[33]

The expedition had made a good beginning, and Duquesne had reason to feel optimistic about its success. But Marin began to have his troubles. His officers and men became restless and dissatisfied. Exhaustion and illness began to take their toll among the men. There

---

[31] Duquesne to Marin, July 22, 1753, Archives du Séminaire de Québec, V-V, 5:62:8.

[32] Duquesne to the Minister, August 20, 1753, *Wilderness Chronicles*, 51-52. The Governor summarized Marin's reply.

[33] *Ibid.*

The probable site of the Halfway Post on the Presque Isle Portage.
—*Pennsylvania Historical and Museum Commission.*

were growing signs of Indian animosity. Late in the summer, unusually dry weather reduced to a mere trickle the stream on which the descent to the Ohio was to have been made. One good rainstorm would have brought enough water to float all his boats and canoes down the creek, but none came, which must indeed have been vexing to the "half-ferocious" commander. And in spite of the dry weather, the French had a great deal of trouble with mud on the portage road. Either because they followed the old Indian path, or because they tried to take the straightest possible course from Presque Isle to Le Boeuf, their road led through swampy, wet ground, although a deviation of a mile or two would have brought them over dry ground. Where the passage of a few moccasined Indians would scarcely have broken the surface, the movement of heavily-laden soldiers and horses and carts quickly broke up the soil and reduced it to mud, so that the unfortunate French Canadians had to wade in it up to their knees.

By August 27 Governor Duquesne knew that Marin was having difficulties with his officers, and wrote to the commander that their discontent was "the subject of daily conversation" in Montreal. "It seems," he said, "that all your subordinate officers . . . were distressed by such a lengthy campaign; that their zeal . . . had totally abated; and that, in truth, if they performed what they were ordered to do, it was only for pure obedience and for fear of . . . punishment . . ."

37

He ordered Marin to watch for the "dejected and discouraged faces" among them, and "to send them to Montreal on the earliest occasion so that I can make an example of them."[34]

It would appear, however, that the commander himself was to blame for much of the dissatisfaction among his officers. Perhaps it was the stress and strain of his many responsibilities, perhaps it was the first sign of the illness which was to kill him, that made him captious and overbearing, inclined to listen to complaints and act hastily. This is illustrated in his dealings with Jean Daniel Dumas, the commander of the camp at Le Boeuf, whom he may have distrusted as a recent newcomer from France.

On August 26, Marin wrote a grumbling letter to Dumas. The engineer Drouillon was not getting enough help in building the fort, and should not be given the additional duty of clearing the creek of the underbrush which impeded navigation. Dumas should assign another officer to that task. Marin threw in a slighting remark in connection with news about the arrival of supplies: "In case there are any whom this arrival of help deprives of all hope of returning this year, and if there is anyone who is not pleased to continue the campaign, you can assure them, Sir, that upon any request they make of me I shall not hesitate to send them back immediately." Further, he complained because Indian news came from Le Boeuf that Dumas had not told him about, and he relayed a complaint of Drouillon "that when he showed you the necessity of benefitting by the first good waters to bring a load of stone aboard every pirogue, you had replied that all these gentlemen had authority to do so, but you could not give them the order, since you had no order from me about it." He scolded, "I am surprised, Sir, that you require orders from me to decide when one requests anything from you for the good of the work, and I hope that in the future it will not happen again."[35]

Dumas answered each point of criticism politely. He said that he knew nothing about any Indians going from Le Boeuf to Presque Isle, denied that he had refused to give orders about bringing stone, and assured the commander that he was trying to cooperate with Drouillon. Le Mercier had left him in doubt whether the entire bed of the stream was to be cleared or only enough for a canoe to pass, and Marin had not answered his previous inquiry about it. He had set La Chauvignerie to work clearing the stream above the fort, as far as Montesson's

---

[34] Duquesne to Marin, August 27, 1753, *Papiers Contrecoeur,* 45; also *Wilderness Chronicles,* 54, from Archives Nationales, C 11 A 99, f. 144.

[35] Marin to Dumas, August 26, 1753, *Papiers Contrecoeur,* 42-43.

boatyard, and would assign De Léry to clear the river below Lake Le Boeuf. In general reply to Marin's criticism, he said, "I am sorry, Sir, that you feel you have any reasons to be displeased with me, and that you left me in ignorance about them. The slightest word from you would have set me straight." Then Dumas took up Marin's slighting remarks about dissatisfied officers: "Since the general leaves you ·free to send back the officers as you think best, I beg you, Sir, to include me in that number. I cannot see that there will be much glory for me in this campaign, and I shall thus avoid the unpleasantnesses of which I am already getting a foretaste."[36]

A day later, in a curt note, Marin relieved him of his command: "Please, Sir, immediately on receiving my letter, turn over the command to M. de Boishebert, to whom I am writing accordingly. . . . I advise you that some canoes will leave for Niagara tomorrow."[37] At the same time, Marin wrote Duquesne that he was sending Dumas to Niagara to await further orders from Péan, and boasted, "I have begun with one of the main officers to stop the progress of the intriguing frame of mind."[38] He told Boishébert, the new commander of Fort Le Boeuf, to "continue having the river cleared, . . . and to take every care that all our works proceed rapidly." "Time is becoming dear,"[39] he concluded, revealing one cause of his bad temper.

Dumas did not, however, remain in disgrace for long, He went, as instructed, to Fort Niagara where he talked with Péan, the second-in-command. This influential man, the friend of Bigot and Duquesne, did not agree with Marin's hasty action. He wrote to intercede for Dumas, and Marin had no choice but to back down. He told Péan that "I shall always approve, my dear friend, what will give pleasure to you," and agreed that his letter to the Governor should be held at Niagara. Of Dumas he said, "He will find me disposed to show him friendship; I hope that his repentance will save others."[40] He even wrote a letter praising Dumas to the Governor, and told Dumas himself, "I should be truly pleased, Sir, to be among the number of your friends."[41]

[36] Dumas to Marin, August 27, 1753, *Papiers Contrecoeur*, 46-48

[37] Marin to Dumas, [August 28, 1753], Archives du Séminaire de Québec, V-V, 5:62:9b.

[38] Marin to Duquesne, August 28, 1753, *Papiers Contrecoeur*, 49-50. Here it is identified as from Marin to Contrecoeur, who did hold it on Marin's later instructions.

[39] Marin to Boishébert, [August 28, 1753], Archives du Séminaire de Québec, V-V, 5:62:10b.

[40] Marin to Péan, undated, Archives du Séminaire de Québec, V-V, 5:62:12b.

[41] Marin to Dumas, undated, Archives du Séminaire de Québec, V-V, 5:62:11b.

This episode reveals Marin's weakness as a commander, for it cannot be doubted that he was inept and unsteady in handling Dumas. Péan's intercession, however, was to be thoroughly justified. Two years later, it was Dumas who rallied the French and Indians to defeat Braddock, winning fame as the "Hero of the Monongahela." It can only be concluded that Marin was unable to get along even with a capable officer—that he stirred up trouble for himself.

Jean-Daniel Dumas.
—*Public Archives of Canada.*

The dissension among the officers had its effect upon the soldiers, who grew tired of the hard work and the unaccustomed discipline. Desertions multiplied. French Canadians had always found it easy to adopt Indian ways and wilderness life, and now the men fled to the villages on the Allegheny, where they received hospitality and protection. An amusing and human story about such a deserter illustrates this point. Joncaire at Venango heard that there was a deserter at the village of Cananouangon, near the present site of Warren, and sent to ask the Indians to bring him back. His letter to Marin on September 12 made the following report:

> The Indians of Cananouangon have sent me word that twice they had sent after the deserter, but he hadn't wanted to go, and said to them, "I know quite well that I am condemned to death. So there is no use promising that nothing will happen to me. I know

40

the contrary. You may kill me and take my scalp to Onontio,[42] in order to inform him that I am dead, because I don't want to go back at all."

Upon realizing this, they had left him because they did not have the heart to kill him.

And that, Sir, is what they informed me.[43]

Far from being bloodthirsty savages, the Indians just could not understand killing a man as punishment for violating civilized military regulations.

In spite of the evidences of declining morale, preparations still continued for the descent to the Belle Rivière. Parties of men had been set to work making pirogues at two boatyards on the Rivière aux Boeufs, one some distance above Fort Le Boeuf, and the other downstream at or near the forks.[44] Late in July Péan had reached Fort Niagara with the rear guard, the last detachment of men, and the final consignment of supplies. On August 14, he came to Presque Isle for a conference with Marin and Le Mercier, but returned to Niagara to superintend the shipment of supplies. It was not until the 8th of September that this task was completed, so that Péan could join Marin. Meanwhile, Marin wrote of his "great pleasure that you ought to arrive here at once." He continued:

> If I had followed my inclination, I should have waited for you, but I am forced to set out by the circumstances we are in. Things are taking a good turn, however, but I saw them on the point of having bad results for the campaign. Upon your arrival I count on your coming to the Fort de la Riviere au Boeuf, so that we shall confer there.[45]

Because of these continuing preparations, the Governor wrote the Minister on October 3 that he thought Péan must have "joined Sieur Marin in the lower reaches of the Riviere au Boeuf during the last days of [September], and that they have journeyed together on the Rivicre d'Oyo." He hoped soon to be "in a position to report the details of that march."[46]

---

[42] The Indian name for the Governor of Canada.

[43] Joncaire to Marin, September 12, 1753, *Papiers Contrecoeur*, 65.

[44] The Rivière aux Boeufs of the French included what we now call Le Boeuf Creek and French Creek below their junction. They thought of the upper part of French Creek as a tributary.

[45] Marin to Péan, undated, Archives du Séminaire de Québec, V-V, 5:61:12b.

[46] Duquesne to the Minister, October 3, 1753, *Wilderness Chronicles*, 55.

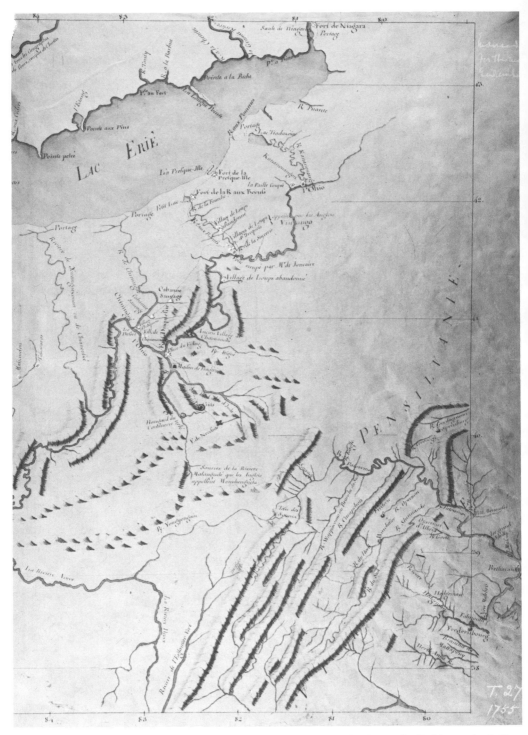

Bellin's Map of the Belle Rivière. Eastern section of *Carte du Cours de l'Ohio ou la Belle Riviere . . .*, Par le Sieur Bellin Ingenieur de la Marine 1755. The legend, on the western section, states: "The Part between Fort Presque-Isle and the Riviere de Chiningué, with the Environs of the Riviere de Malenguelé, has been drawn from plans and memoirs of the Chevalier le Mercier."

—*Public Archives of Canada.*

THE HALF KING WARNS THE FRENCH

Whatever else might delay or halt the French invasion of the Belle Rivière, there were few signs of human opposition in its opening stages. No early action was to be expected from the British colonies, for—as Duquesne put it—"to raise an English troop more time and threats are necessary than for levying Canadians."[1] Meanwhile, the Indians were impressed and overawed by the French forces, and hesitant about seeming to oppose them. Some idea of the effect of this movement of troops on the Indian mind may be gathered from the remarks of one Indian who returned to his village near Montreal after sixteen years' absence: "He said he was coming to embrace the Christian religion with all his heart in order to get on the right road, and that the earth was trembling from the multitude of French who were at the Riviere au Boeuf. Besides that, he said with a frightened look, they are holding hands from Presquisle to La Chine."[2]

The French agents and traders on the Belle Rivière had done a good advance job, lulling Indian suspicions, giving them to understand that the French were coming only to help them, and keeping watch on English activities. Captain Joncaire had shifted his base of operations from Chiningué to the upper Allegheny, to the Paille Coupée—Cananouangon villages, where his influence as an adopted Seneca could be most effective. The bountiful cornfields of the Cananouangon region, on the fertile meadows above and below Warren, would be a granary for the French forces, if these Indians could be kept quiet and friendly. In the meantime, La Saussaye, Montisambert, and other French traders at Chiningué looked after French interests among the Indians of the lower valley.[3]

In the early spring, Joncaire could assure Duquesne, with some degree of certainty, that there was "perfect quiet along the Belle Rivière on the part of his Indians."[4] In April, Duquesne told Contrecoeur that "the king was not very eager to humor the Iroquois, still less

---

[1] Duquesne to Marin, June 13, 1753, Archives du Séminaire de Québec, V-V, 5:62:5.

[2] Duquesne to Marin, July 10, 1753, Archives du Séminaire de Québec, V-V, 5:62:6.

[3] In 1752 La Saussaye had a dispute of some sort with Montisambert, and went back to Montreal to present his case to the Governor. Duquesne sent him to Marin in July, 1753, with permission to look after his business interests. Joncaire to Baby, March 11, 1752, Université de Montréal, Collection Baby; Duquesne to Marin, July 10, 1753, Archives du Séminaire de Québec, V-V, 5:62:6.

[4] Duquesne to Contrecoeur, March 19, 1753, *Papiers Contrecoeur*, 24-26.

to notify them in advance about the new establishments that his Majesty wants to make along the Belle Riviere." However, news of the expedition had "so well penetrated the Upper Country" that he thought it best to have Contrecoeur present a wampum belt to the Iroquois of the Niagara portage "to warn them only that I am going to settle on the Belle Riviere as on land that belongs to me without question."[5] The chief of the Niagara Iroquois received this belt and message in a "grateful way," and it even appeared that "the Five Nations did not want to attend the council of the English to which they were invited."[6] On the first of July, the Governor could say with satisfaction, "From the news reaching me from everywhere, the Indians are trembling and ask only for clemency."[7]

The Junction of French Creek with the Allegheny River.
—*Pennsylvania Historical and Museum Commission.*

The attitude of the Iroquois Confederacy, historically the enemy of French Canada and the ally of the English, was of special importance, since they claimed ownership of the Belle Rivière country, and were in a position to interfere with the French line of communications. Long years of effort by the Governors of New France and by the Joncaires now seemed likely to bring them to the French side, or at least to keep them neutral. The French expedition by its seemingly overwhelming force overawed the Iroquois, and led them to take an un-

---

[5] Duquesne to Contrecoeur, April 14, 1753, *Papiers Contrecoeur*, 31-32.

[6] Duquesne to Contrecoeur, June 1, 1753, Archives du Séminaire de Québec, V-V, 1:18.

[7] Duquesne to Contrecoeur, July 1, 1753, Archives du Séminaire de Québec, V-V, 1:21.

usual measure.   In June of 1753, they sent their matriarchs to Fort
Presque Isle to ask Marin what the French were going to do.

In the words of Duquesne's report to the Minister,

> The only step they have taken has been to send the Ladies (Dames)
> of their Council, to inquire of him, by a Belt, whether he was march-
> ing with the hatchet uplifted, or to establish tranquility. This Com-
> mander answered them, that when he marched with the hatchet, he
> bore it aloft, in order that no person should be ignorant of the fact,
> but as for the present, his orders were to use it only in case he en-
> countered opposition to my will; that my intention was to support
> and assist them in their necessities, and to drive away the evil spirits
> that encompassed them and disturbed the earth.[8]

The Governor and Marin undoubtedly understood the significance
of the Iroquois women taking an active part in affairs, that those who
had the primary right to speak in matters involving land, war, and
peace wished to avoid hostile action.   From the Governor's tone it is
implied that they did raise cautious objections to the French invasion,
but did not press them.   In a letter to Marin, the Governor expressed
his satisfaction with "the trembling speeches of the Ladies of the
Council" and with Marin's reply "like a brave warrior to the lifted
hatchet when at war."   He had "no doubt that it made an impression
on them."[9]   From other sources the Governor heard that the Iroquois
were rejecting English overtures for action against the invasion:

> They answered that they would not meddle with my affairs, and
> that they would look quietly on, from their mats, persuaded, as they
> were, that my proceedings had no other object than to give a clear
> sky to a country which served as a refuge for assassins who had red-
> dened the ground with blood.[10]

About the same time, Joncaire and Montisambert came to report on
the way things looked at Paille Coupée and Chiningué, and to give
the commander advice and help in his dealings with the Indians.   Joncaire arrived with some Loups (Delawares), probably from their villages on lower French Creek, and Marin wrote Contrecoeur on June 27,
"I am very tranquil about events on the Belle Rivière where everyone
appears very well disposed."[11]   These visitors from the lesser tribes of
the Belle Rivière, the Loups and Shawnees who lived there under
Iroquois protection, were treated with especial liberality.   Marin's

---

[8] Duquesne to the Minister, August 20, 1753, *Wilderness Chronicles,* 50-51.

[9] Duquesne to Marin, July 10, 1753, Archives du Séminaire de Québec, V-V, 5:62:6.
This meeting must have taken place shortly before June 26, since the Governor
acknowledged a letter of that date.

[10] Duquesne to the Minister August 20, 1753, *Wilderness Chronicles,* 51.

[11] Marin to Contrecoeur, June 27, 1753, Archives du Séminaire de Québec, V-V,
1:63.

account of his entertainment of two of these Indians amused the Governor so much that he wrote:

> If you clean up all the Indians who come to see you as thoroughly as you cleaned up your two Loups in order to refresh them, I expect, Mr. Commander, that you will always have cleaning jobs on hand; and I shall no longer be troubled when they meet you, that you have no experience.
>
> Stopping the fun which I have had in writing this, I approve your liberality very strongly; that is what is called sowing in order to reap.[12]

The Governor told Marin, "Leave them all in complete freedom, and assure them that you would like very much to serve as their arbitrator, but that if they do any evil deeds without your knowledge, I shall crush them."[13] He advised the commander "to receive with kindness all my children who may come to you and who may have recourse to your meditation," and was so optimistic about the effects of the expedition that he remarked, "There is an appearance that you will be the Angel of Peace of the Belle Riviere."[14]

Many of the Indians thought only of making what profit they could from the expedition, coming to get presents in their accustomed manner. Many of them earned trade goods, food, and ammunition by carrying on the portages or by hiring out their horses. They sold the Frenchmen corn, and went hunting to get them fresh meat. The Niagara portage had long been a regular source of income to the Indians of that locality, and now the Presque Isle portage offered another golden opportunity to the Belle Rivière Indians, who came from Venango and from far down the Allegheny in search of work.

The only openly expressed opposition to the French invasion of the Belle Rivière came from the Iroquois of the lower Allegheny region, led by the Half King Tanacharison. This vivid and dynamic old Indian was the leader of the Senecas and representative of the Six Nations in that region, but he did not hesitate to take a virtually independent line when the Confederacy itself took a neutral position. There were other leaders or "regents" of the Six Nations in the Ohio country, but the force of the Half King's personality, his initiative, and his native ability, which are so apparent in the Journals of the young George Washington, put him in the forefront of the efforts to halt or delay the French. Bound by treaties and by trading interests with the British colonies of Pennsylvania and Virginia, these Indians could not help but regard the French movements with anxiety, and

---

[12] Duquesne to Marin, July 10, 1753, Archives du Séminaire de Québec, V-V, 5:62:6.

[13] *Ibid.*

[14] *Ibid.*

they had had assurances of Virginian support. As early as May, the Half King had assured English traders at Pine Creek "that they would be safe under their Protection while they are safe themselves."[15] Now he was to be the only Indian to oppose the French openly, the only inhabitant of the Belle Rivière to speak out boldly against the invasion of his land.

In the opening days of September, the Half King and other Indians representing the tribes of the Ohio country came to Presque Isle to hold council with the French. Joncaire had already written Marin a word of caution:

> The man named Thaninhison[16] is the one who is to speak in the council which is to be held at your place. He was formerly inclined to the French, but at present he is more English than the English, working only against the French by continually saying foolish things. In a word, he is no good, and it is he who sold the lands to the English. This man is from the Lake of Two Mountains,[17] and wants to manage everything in his own way, listening to no one.[18]

On September 2, the first day of the Council at Presque Isle, the Half King emphasized that he and his following did not represent the Iroquois Confederacy, in these words: "My father, these are warriors and not chiefs who come to bid you good day." Further discussion was postponed until the next day, as he said that "business should never be hurried."[19]

On September 3, the Council resumed its session, and the Half King made a lengthy speech, explaining his position, and begging the French not to invade his country.

> My father, evil tidings are innumerable in the lands where we live. The river where we are belongs to us warriors. The chiefs who look after (public) affairs are not its masters.[20] It is a road for warriors and not for these chiefs. M. de Joncaire came there three years ago with much merchandise which he distributed as he pleased, after which he said that he had acquired the land as far as the Rivière au Boeuf, and that troubled me. I would like, my father,

---

[15] Report on French Activities, May 25, 1753, *Wilderness Chronicles*, 75-76.

[16] A French form of Tanacharison.

[17] That is, he came from the Christianized Mohawk village on the lake formed by the widening of the Ottawa River at its mouth, above the Island of Montreal. It may be Joncaire's indirect way of saying, "This no-good is a backslider from one of our Christian Indian villages."

[18] Joncaire to Marin, undated, Archives du Séminaire de Québec, V-V, 5:60:2.

[19] Council Held by the Sonontouans Come from Belle Rivière, September 2, 1753, *Papiers Contrecoeur*, 53-58.

[20] By this he meant that the Council at Onondago, the governing body of the Six Nations, did not own the Belle Rivière country—that it belonged to the people who lived there.

to know your feelings about this. We were told that you were coming with quantities of goods, just as M. de Joncaire came before, and that you were coming to take pity on your children. We think that when you have dressed us up, you will say that the land has been paid for.[21]

The Half King claimed that he had prevented his people from attacking the French during the previous war:

These past years when you were at war with the English, the blows that Onontio[22] dealt reached as far as our cabins. All the warriors wanted to go strike at Detroit. It is I who prevented the blows, and they tell you, my father, that I am a bad man. I thought I did well. You know, my father, that the blows which the Five Nations deal are heavy, and if I had wanted to let them go ahead, they would have broken Onontio's head.

"I alone opposed it,"[23] he said.

Then he turned to the subject of the English traders whom the French had arrested and sent to Montreal, although the Half King had promised them protection:

My father, I show you a peace treaty you made with the English when the war was over. We thought that this treaty was settled. However, we see that six of them have been taken this winter. Now you have taken two more from the R. au Beûf. That is what makes us think that peace has not been made.

The English have told us that they were surprised to see that we let their people be taken whom we ourselves had brought, but that they did not want to declare war since the land was not theirs.[24]

The Half King was slow in coming to the main point of his speech, and first seemed to imply that he might acquiesce in the French occupation of the Belle Rivière:

My father, we come today to learn your feelings since we are accused of selling the land. We beg you to tell us in whose name you are coming to set up these establishments. If it is you, my father, who come to settle in the name of your chief, you will please tell us, for then we shall be calm.

I am speaking, my father, in the name of all the warriors who inhabit the Belle Rivière. We come to learn your sentiments so that we can calm down our wives. We have learned that you were too heavily loaded down to travel with speed. That is why we decided to come and meet you.[25]

---

[21] Council Held by the Sonontouans, September 2, 1753, *Papiers Contrecoeur*, 53-58.

[22] The Indian name for the Governor of Canada.

[23] Council Held by the Sonontouans, September 2, 1753, *Papiers Contrecoeur*, 53-58.

[24] *Ibid.* The two captured traders were John Trotter and his man; see Trent's Journal, in Mary C. Darlington, ed., *History of Colonel Henry Bouquet*, 39. Their arrest is mentioned in Marin to Contrecoeur, August 17, 1753, *Papiers Contrecoeur*, 41.

[25] Council Held by the Sonontouans, *loc. cit.*

He spoke of past troubles between the French and the Iroquois:

My father, we are going to speak of the first councils we held. When peace was made between you and us, our father . . . pledged us to forget the evil deeds, and that, if there were any who were evil-minded, he would invite us all to chastise whoever would do evil and to take the bad hatchet from him, and that he would throw it into a deep well . . . in which it was impossible to find it again.[26]

Seeming to gain confidence as he spoke, the Half King finally dared to warn the French commander:

We remember well what our father said, and we impressed it on our memory. With this belt we detain you and ask you to have them cease setting up the establishments you want to make. All the tribes have always called upon us not to allow it. We have told our brothers the English to withdraw. They have done so, too. We shall be on the side of those who take pity on us and who listen to us. Although I am small, the Master of Life has not given me less courage to oppose these establishments. This is the first and last demand we shall make of you, and I shall strike at whoever does not listen to us.

With these four strings of wampum, we tell you that we ask you to listen to the request we make of you and to the opposition we have to the establishment on our river. We therefore ask you, my father, to take pity on our children and those to come, seeing that, if you settle here, it is the way to make us all perish. We ask you only to send there what we need, but not to build any forts there.[27]

Thus, two months before the Governor of Virginia sent notice of trespass to the French, the Half King as spokesman for native inhabitants of the Ohio country warned the French not to come down the Allegheny. His speech on September 3, 1753, was the first formal objection to the French invasion.

Marin's reply was stern and unyielding. He refused to accept the wampum belts and strings, thus technically refusing to hear the speech, and told the Half King that his Indians seemed "like people who have lost their minds." He declared that "The establishments which I am setting up and which I shall continue along the Belle Rivière are founded on the fact that it belongs incontestably to the King," and

---

[26] *Ibid.*

[27] *Ibid.* It is interesting to compare this with the Half King's own account of his speech, as given to Washington on November 25, 1753. In recollection, his language became even bolder, as illustrated by the following passage: "If you had come in a peaceable Manner, like our Brothers, the *English*, we should not have been against your trading with us, as they do; BUT TO COME, FATHERS, AND BUILD HOUSES UPON OUR LAND, AND TO TAKE IT BY FORCE, IS WHAT WE CANNOT SUBMIT TO." Fitzpatrick, ed., *The Diaries of George Washington*, I, 48.

disclaimed any intention of "wishing to disturb the nations who live along the Belle Riviere." On the contrary, he said,

> We want only to protect them, to help them with their necessities, and to chase away the evil spirits who surround them and are very anxious to put them on the wrong track. His Majesty has ordered these establishments in order to be assured of the faithfulness of his children, and His Majesty leaves them complete freedom to go and trade their furs wherever they think best. This was already announced to your village beginning in the spring, and I repeated it to all who came here.[28]

To the Half King's demand that the French not enter the Belle Rivière country, Marin retorted,

> I despise all the stupid things you said. I know that they come only from you, and that all the warriors and chiefs of the Belle Rivière think better than you, and take pity on their women and children. I am obliged to tell you that I shall continue on my way, and if there are any persons bold enough to set up barriers to hinder my march, I shall knock them over so vigorously that they may crush those who made them.

He admonished him, "Therefore, consider all this carefully. Perhaps you will come to your senses and recognize your folly and the risk you have been running."[29]

The Half King brought the Council to an end with a calm and dignified statement:

> My father, I have no comment to make on what you say to me. You can well believe that I do not come from my chief. I am sent by the nations which I named this morning.[30] It will be up to them to decide what they will do. This is the third refusal you have given me.[31]

Despite the assurance of the French commander's words, the Half King did give him cause to worry. Marin wrote to Joncaire about this

---

[28] Council Held by the Sonontouans, *loc. cit.*

[29] *Ibid.* The Half King's version of Marin's reply is in Fitzpatrick, ed., *The Diaries of George Washington*, I, 49. The substance of it was, "I tell you, down the River I will go. . . . Child, you talk foolish; you say this Land belongs to you, but there is not the Black of my Nail yours."

[30] The nations are not named in the record; probably he said Sonontouans (Senecas), Loups (Delawares), and Chaouanons (Shawnees). A letter from Joncaire to Marin before the Council (Archives du Séminaire de Québec, V-V, 5:60:2) implies that there were Loups in attendance, for the pro-French chief of the Loups at Venango was annoyed that his people did not inform him about it. Later, the Chaouanons took pains to dissociate themselves from the Half King's stand.

[31] Council Held by the Sonontouans, *loc. cit.* As to the two earlier refusals, one of the Half King's people had talked with the French in July, and Scaruneate (Scaroyady) and other deputies had been to Presque Isle in August: see Trent's Journal, *op. cit.*, 20-21, 35-38.

"insolent fellow," how the Half King had come to Presque Isle and "talked as badly as possible." "I rejected his words," Marin said, and then added dubiously, "I am told that he has little repute among the nations. You will be so kind as to inform me about it and tell me what the result of his action will be. If it were possible for you to send me some one of his nation to contradict him, it would do a world of good."[32]

Drawing of a Lead Seal recovered at the site of Fort Le Boeuf.
—Pennsylvania Historical and Museum Commission.

In fact, the Half King seems to have had very little backing, except from his own group of Ohio Iroquois, whom he referred to as the "warriors." When the delegates from the Shawnees spoke to the French on the following day, they denied any part in what the Half King had said. "We think much better," they explained, "all the more because we are not capable of resisting and because we take pity on our women and children." They assured the French of their faithfulness, and even welcomed them, "We shall be as glad to see you in our village as you seem to be to hear us speak."[33] This may have been in the hope of getting the customary presents—perhaps, too, with the thought of freeing themselves from the domination of the Iroquois. Later, the Half King's stand was disavowed by the Council of the Six Nations, and he was even reprimanded. He seems to have realized in advance that this would happen, for he had said specifically that he came from the warriors, not from the chiefs.

Duperont Baby, the French trader and agent at Chiningué (Logstown), had already reported to Joncaire that "All the Indians are murmuring a great deal about Onontio's undertaking."[34] Now the Half King returned to Chiningué, determined to do all he could to stir up resistance to the French, and full of wrath against the Shawnees. As Baby put it,

> The Iroquois are grumbling loudly because the Cha8enons did not speak with M. de Marin with as much insolence as they did.

---

[32] Marin to Joncaire, undated, *Papiers Contrecoeur,* 58-59.

[33] Speech of the Cha8oinons, September 4, 1753, *Papiers Contrecoeur,* 61-62.

[34] Joncaire to Marin, September 12, 1753, *Papiers Contrecoeur,* 65-67.

They incessantly reproach them, and out of spite—I have heard it said from different sources—they would not delay in striking a blow at the French. They have even wanted to leave already, but I do not know what reasons stopped them. I think they are waiting for the arrival of those who went to the English.[35]

At the same time that the delegation headed by the Half King went to Presque Isle, another group had gone with Trent and Montour to Virginia.

Baby also reported that "Immediately upon the arrival of *Thanenhison*[36] [the Half King], the English traders withdrew on his advice, and they are still leaving every day. It is said that they are making big preparations and will not be long in arriving in great numbers."[37]

The Shawnees were still well-satisfied with their independent move, while the Iroquois were becoming increasingly annoyed. Baby described the situation:

The Cha8enons are not making much noise. They are very much pleased with M. Marin. They await him with great impatience. As for the Iroquois, they are of a different opinion, and if the rumor is true, it will not be long before you hear from them, as I pointed out above—and all because of the advice of Thanenhison who wants to achieve his purposes.[38]

Without a great deal of real backing, the Half King had put up a good bluff at the Presque Isle Council. Now the gloomy reports from Chiningué, that the Iroquois were threatening to take action and "block the road," made the situation on the Belle Rivière look very treacherous to the French commander. It is too much to say that this alone kept the French from advancing farther in the fall of 1753, but the Half King's warning did help to cause that decision.

---

[35] Duperont Baby to Marin, September 5 (?), 1753, *Papiers Contrecoeur*, 63.

[36] Underlined in the original.

[37] Duperont Baby to Marin, *loc. cit.*

[38] *Ibid.*

NATURE DELAYS THE FRENCH

If the Half King had' added to his eloquent speech a curse, if he had summoned the spirits of earth and air and water to smite the invaders, he might well have claimed credit for their ensuing troubles. The forces of nature, as manifested by disease, fatigue, and the weather, combined to halt the campaign of 1753 at the very threshold of the Belle Rivière.

More serious than Indian hostility, or tired men and discontented officers, or dry weather and muddy roads, was the outbreak of illness and disease among the troops. Exhausting labor, lack of shelter, and a badly balanced diet combined with eighteenth century ignorance of sanitary and health measures to wreck the French army more overwhelmingly than a military defeat. Scurvy, fevers, pneumonia, and dysentery wrought havoc in the ranks and among the officers.

By the middle of the summer, illness had become prevalent enough among the troops to be a matter of concern in the conference which Marin, Péan, and Le Mercier held at Presque Isle on August 14. Because of this, and because they feared their provisions might run low, they decided to send the invalids back to Canada with enough more to bring the total of the expeditionary force down to 1350 men. After his return to Niagara, Péan had the sick there examined, and sent 242 men on board two barks for the return journey to Fort Frontenac and Montreal. Later in August, Marin decided to send back only the sick men from his camps, but they already numbered three hundred.[1]

A gradual increase of illness is shown in various letters during August. On the 17th, Marin told Contrecoeur, "Our work is going well, but we are not without having some sick men. For several days I have been one of them, but I am getting better."[2] In a letter from Montreal on August 18, Varin alluded to the sick rate at Fort Niagara: "It is unfortunate that scurvy and fevers are breaking out so considerably, and it is to be hoped that the precaution you have taken to put the patients under tents in the garden has prevented the

---

[1] Severance, *Old Frontier of France*, II, 12, 17. Severance based his account on Péan's letters and on the *Mémoire* presented at Péan's trial, but his citations are somewhat imprecise. Péan's return from Presque Isle is mentioned in Varin to Contrecoeur, August 27, 1753, *Papiers Contrecoeur*, 48-49.

[2] Marin to Contrecoeur, August 17, 1753, *Papiers Contrecoeur*, 41.

spread of the disease."[3] On August 27, Varin wrote again to Contrecoeur, "You have done well to send back the sick people. Two have already died, and there are others dying. You should not keep them at Niagara for long. They were very badly cared for at Presque Isle by Sieur Vitre. M. du Breuil[4] has arrived and is much better at present."[5] About the same time, Marin himself was wondering how he could possibly supply Péan with "fifty canoes with crews of nine men each, which will make 450 men, . . . considering those who are not in shape to carry."[6] By the end of the month of August, both Montesson and De Léry were too ill for duty at Le Boeuf, and Marin sent his sympathy to them in a letter to Boishébert, the commander there.[7]

During the summer, however, the leaders did not seem to feel that sickness would threaten the success of their campaign. It was quite the usual thing to have some sick soldiers, and if the proportion were greater than usual, that could be ascribed to the unusually heavy work in carrying on the portages and in building the forts. They pressed ahead with their preparations for the descent of the Rivière aux Boeufs. This involved the building of enough pirogues to carry the army and its supplies; the exploration of the stream, if possible removing any obstacles to navigation; and arranging for an advance base at Venango, where the Rivière aux Boeufs (French Creek) enters the Allegheny.

The building of pirogues was begun as early as August 7, when Marin accepted an offer from Montesson to go and build pirogues, and assigned eight to ten men for the job.[8] It is apparent from Dumas's letter of August 27 that Montesson's boatyard was on Le Boeuf Creek above the fort, for he said: "M. de la Chauvignerie is working on clearing the upper river, so that M. de Montesson's pirogues can go down."[9] De Léry was to leave Fort Le Boeuf on August 28 "to go to the forks to find out about obstructions in the river on the way down."[10]

---

[3] Varin to Contrecoeur, August 18, 1753, Archives du Séminaire de Québec, V-V, 4:311.

[4] La Corne du Breuil, with La Chauvignerie, had reconnoitered the portage to Le Boeuf in June. He died in Quebec in October, 1753, probably from illness contracted on the campaign.

[5] Varin to Contrecoeur, August 27, 1753, Papiers Contrecoeur, 48-49.

[6] Marin to Duquesne, August 28, 1753, Papiers Contrecoeur, 49-50.

[7] Marin to Boishébert, August 30, 1753, Papiers Contrecoeur, 51. (Erroneously identified as written to Contrecoeur.)

[8] Marin to [Montesson], August 7, 1753, Archives du Séminaire de Québec, V-V, 5:60:9.

[9] Dumas to Marin, August 27, 1753, Papiers Contrecoeur, 46-48.

[10] Ibid.

About the same time, Marin told Boishébert, "Please continue having the river cleared, just as I told you here, and take every care that all our works proceed rapidly."[11] On August 30, he told him:

> As soon as the men at M. de Montesson's boatyard have finished putting the bars on their pirogues, I beg you to order them to help our gentlemen finish theirs.
>
> We shall give them a helping hand after the first rains to have these first ones go down.
>
> You will please express to M. de Bayeul the little satisfaction I feel at not being able to count on what he said concerning the pirogues, and beg him for me to be more circumspect in the reports he gives me.
>
> You will please oblige me, Sir, by having a new visit made along the river to see if we cannot discover more trees to make pirogues. Even if it were two or three leagues farther on, that would not be an objection.[12]

From this letter it is evident that more pirogues were being built at another boatyard below the fort, on Le Boeuf Creek or French Creek. For some reason, too, Marin was annoyed by Bayeul's reports which apparently had something to do with the pirogues, either the rate at which they could be made, or the amount of wood available for making them. The fact that criticism of Bayeul is coupled with orders for a new visit along the stream implies, however, that Bayeul had made an earlier trip down the Rivière aux Boeufs. This trip may possibly be connected with an incident related by Stephen Coffin.

In his deposition, Stephen Coffin said that a "Mons.ʳ Bite" was sent by Marin to visit the mouth of the Rivière aux Boeufs. It is conceivable that he actually said "Bile" for Bayeul, and that the clerk who took down his statement accidentally crossed the "l."[13] According to Coffin, "Bite" talked with the Indians at "Ganagarah-hare," or Venango, and on his return trip captured two English traders, who were "bound and brought Prisoners to Morang."[14] The Half King mentioned these captured Englishmen in his speech on September 3,[15] and on the same day Governor Duquesne wrote of

---

[11] Marin to Boishébert, c. August 28, 1753, Archives du Séminaire de Québec, V-V, 5:62:10b.

[12] Marin to Boishébert, August 30, 1753, *Papiers Contrecoeur*, 51.

[13] This is not a mere typographical error in the printed versions of the deposition.

[14] Examination of Stephen Coffin, January 10, 1754, Sir William Johnson Manuscripts, Vol. 23, p. 170. New York State Library; Deposition of Stephen Coffen, Provincial Record, M, 304-307, printed in *Wilderness Chronicles*, 43-45; *Colonial Records*, VI, 9-10.

[15] See page 48, note 24.

their arrival at Montreal.[16] Coffin continued that "the said Bite reported to Morang the Situation was good, but the Water in the river O Baff too Low at that time to carry down any Craft with provisions &ᶜᵃ"[17] If it is correct to suppose that "Bite" was Bayeul, what really annoyed Marin in Bayeul's reports "concerning the pirogues" was that there was not enough water to float them.

If there was no such report, or if Marin was not convinced by it, he was soon to hear of low water in the Rivière aux Boeufs from an unimpeachable source, when Captain Joncaire moved from his station at the Indian village of Paille Coupée to Venango. The chief Indian agent of the French would be in a better position there to manage the Loup Indians whose village was nearby; and his new post would also be an advance base for the expedition. The change was planned well in advance. On August 16, Joncaire wrote from Paille Coupée: "I sent off a pirogue to the Rivierre au Boeuf on the 15th of this month; as soon as those who took it return, I shall set off to go there." In a postscript, he added, "The 21st or 22nd, I shall be at the Rivierre au Boeuf."[18]

However, Joncaire did not reach Venango at the mouth of the Rivière aux Boeufs until August 28, "after taking five days to cut a road with mattocks," so that he told Marin, "I have every reason to remember it."[19] At Venango he took over the trading post of John Fraser—cabins, storehouses, and blacksmith shop. Of this he said, "There are two [buildings] still occupied by the Loups. They say they were given to them by the former proprietor."[20]

To the hope expressed by Marin that Joncaire might send pirogues for the expedition, the Indian agent gave a discouraging reply: "Sir, not only can I not send pirogues for lack of men, but there is not enough water to accommodate the vessels which are here."[21]

Joncaire went on to ask for supplies, and to explain his difficulties: "We would need iron and nails, and supplies for those who are up-country, for we have been living on nothing but grain and water for more than a month. It is really a bad spot. Here is a war party arriving." He stopped writing, and went to talk to the Indians, then returned to his letter: "As I noticed that they had some requests to

---

[16] Duquesne to Marin, September 3, 1753, *Papiers Contrecoeur*, 60-61.

[17] Examination of Stephen Coffin, *loc. cit.*

[18] Joncaire to Marin, August 16, 1753, Archives du Séminaire de Québec, V-V, 5:60:1.

[19] Joncaire to Marin, September 1, 1753, *Papiers Contrecoeur*, 52-53.

[20] *Ibid.*

[21] *Ibid.*

make, I hastened to tell them that I had nothing, that they were to be pitied because you were not yet here, that only you could make presents. That is how I got rid of them."[22]

On September 12, Joncaire reported:

> Two Englishmen have appeared here who came to seek their profits which were in the hands of the Indians. They were here about an hour. Though without orders, if I had had any man to guard them, I would have detained them until I had informed you about it.
>
> Two others have gotten free. They had been sent on behalf of the former proprietor of the houses which are here, to drive out the Loups and, if they did not wish to come out, set the buildings on fire. He had been told that I was not there, and the Loups said that he had not given me all the buildings. Thus they saw that they belonged to me, and so there will be a place to store a large quantity of goods.[23]

By sending men to try to destroy his old trading post at Venango, John Fraser had really done a favor for his old friend Joncaire.[24] After that, the Indians could no longer claim that the buildings had been given to them. Joncaire was well pleased, and told Marin, "All the buildings here are very good. I am waiting for some iron to have them all fastened tightly."[25]

Meanwhile, the troops under Marin and Péan were continuing to transport supplies, provisions, and ammunition over the portage from Presque Isle to Fort Le Boeuf, while disease and illness became even more prevalent among the tired and exhausted men. About the middle of September, Marin wrote from Le Boeuf to an officer at Presque Isle:

> It appeared to me, Sir, from the number you indicated to me today, that many men must not be carrying at all. I am not unaware, Sir, that if some abuses occur, they are not by your intention. I have seen them for myself, when at Presqu'ile. But please make all these gentlemen give you exact rolls of everyone who can carry, and not one shall be exempt. I have no need of asking you to leave on guard only persons who are not in shape to carry.[26]

---

[22] *Ibid.*

[23] Joncaire to Marin, September 12, 1753, *Papiers Contrecoeur,* 65-67.

[24] While he was at Venango, John Fraser must have become well acquainted with Joncaire. That the two men were friends is indicated by a letter from Joncaire to Fraser, March 6, 1755, Papers of the Shippen Family, I, 171. HSP. Joncaire said, "I think that the difficulties between us will not destroy in any way the friendship which has existed between us."

[25] Joncaire to Marin, September 12, 1753, *Papiers Contrecoeur,* 65-67.

[26] Letter from Marin, undated, Archives du Séminaire de Québec, V-V, 5:62:13b. Marin acknowledged a letter of September 14.

It is not surprising that the men should have tried to escape the work of the portage. Even in August, Péan had described the toil of the carrying places and its effects on the troops in extreme terms, "It is terrible work. Conceive, Monsieur, that all the carts which you see pass your windows pass over the bodies of men already half dead."[27] Later, he said, "The roads were covered with the sweat of our militia."[28]

The Presque Isle Portage in 1938. Here the portage road veered from the modern highway (which still is called locally, the Old French Road), and descended into the valley of Mill Creek. The trail is no longer visible, because of a fill.

—*Pennsylvania Historical and Museum Commission.*

The movement of troops and carts over the Presque Isle portage reduced the soft, marshy soil to bottomless mire, so that a new roadway had to be made beside the old one. In the words of Péan's *Mémoire,*

The labor of our troops was excessive. The soldiers, sunk half-leg deep in the mud, and weakened by the recent fatigues of the first portage [at Niagara], succumbed under their burdens. It was impossible to use the few horses that remained. It was an afflicting spectacle to behold these debilitated men, struggling at the same time against the bad season and the difficulties of the road, broken

---

[27] Péan to Duquesne, c. August 16, 1753, cited in Severance, *An Old Frontier of France*, II, 14.

[28] *Mémoire pour Michel-Jean-Hugues Péan*, 59, quoted in Frégault, *Bigot*, II, 67.

down by the weight of their weapons and of the loads which they had to carry.[29]

The leaders attributed the increase of illness among the troops to the exhausting labor of the portages, but this was certainly not the sole cause. Scurvy is mentioned repeatedly as the chief ailment. This and other "deficiency" diseases are caused by a lack of certain vitamins in the diet. Among their symptoms are physical exhaustion and mental depression, and in extreme stages they may involve hemorrhages, lung trouble, and intestinal disorders.[30] The "deficiency" diseases could account for all the ailments reported, for the general exhaustion of the men broken by fever and spitting blood,[31] for "fevers and lung diseases,"[32] and even for the hemorrhage Marin suffered.[33] Of course, it may be assumed that dysentery, pneumonia, and other diseases also afflicted the weakened men, but there seems little doubt that a deficient diet was the primary cause of sickness.

Doubtless, Marin and Péan would have scoffed at the idea that the soldiers' rations of salt pork and biscuit ("hard tack") were to blame for the steadily increasing sick rate. But even during the first outbreak of illness in the summer, the obscure gunner J. C. B., as commissary's clerk at Fort Presque Isle, had given himself a striking demonstration of the dietary causes of the soldiers' illness.

"I saw with reluctance," he wrote many years later, "that we were reduced to letting the sick suffer and die with nothing but medicine to help them. Troubled by their suffering, I resolved to break the rules, and undertook to relieve a number of the sick men, if I could not cure them. I adopted twenty-two, asking them to promise the utmost secrecy about the comforts that I was going to procure them, to which they readily agreed."[34]

The interesting point, however, is that the men whom he fed, recovered.

---

[29] *Mémoire pour Michel-Jean-Hugues Péan,* quoted by Severance, *An Old Frontier of France,* II, 19.

[30] See the articles on Scurvy, Vitamins, and Pellagra in the *Encyclopedia Britannica* (Fourteenth Edition).

[31] *Mémoire pour Michel-Jean-Hugues Péan,* 26, cited by Frégault, *Bigot,* II, 66.

[32] Duquesne to the Minister, November 29, 1753, *Wilderness Chronicles,* 60-62.

[33] Duquesne to the Minister, November 2, 1753, *Wilderness Chronicles,* 58-60.

[34] *Travels in New France by J. C. B.,* 32. J. C. B. said that he was a gunner, that his nickname was Jolicoeur (p. 15), and that he took part in the Ohio expedition of 1755 (p. 69). On the roll of "canoniers" in the detachment which left Montreal on March 3, 1755, there is listed Jolicoeur Charles Bonin. *Papiers Contrecoeur,* 278-279. His memoirs were written many years later, and cannot often be reconciled with actual dates and events.

"Each day," he continued, "I put aside bread, wine, and brandy, as well as fresh game. . . . This was the less likely to be missed or noticed, as I often gave them to the Indians who were sent out hunting and scouting. I had the satisfaction of seeing my patients improve daily, and at the end of a fortnight they were quite convalescent. Four or five of the others were buried each day. These I should like to have given the same care; but this I could not do without risking the loss of my position."[35]

As an anti-scorbutic diet, J. C. B.'s prescription was not ideal, but his diet list did include enough sources of life-giving vitamins to save the few men he had selected.

It can hardly be supposed that in his privileged position the commander himself would have been limited to the rations of the troops. In fact, the Governor had teased Marin in June about rumors that he was "living as magnificently as a Marshal of France in command of an army."[36] Nevertheless, the elderly commander became seriously ill in late September, perhaps overcome by the weight of his responsibilities and by premonitions of the failure of his campaign. Duquesne was informed, by a letter of September 29 from Péan, that "Marin was at the last extremity from a hemorrhage which so exhausted him" that his recovery was doubtful. The Governor reported to the Minister: "Immediately I sent out Sieur de St. Pierre, who returns from the Western Sea, to take command of the Belle Riviere and its dependencies, as this officer is the only one in the colony who is capable of replacing [Marin] so as to make himself feared and respected by the Indians."[37]

On October 14, the Governor wrote to the stricken commander:

I am, Sir, infinitely touched by the sad plight into which your very zeal has driven you, as I know you have a temperament which does not lack resources, and as I fear that mental preoccupation will lead to your death. I take so keen an interest in prolonging your days that I do not hesitate to send you Sieur de St. Pierre whom I have ordered to assist you in every way until your complete convalescence.

I hope with all my heart that the officer whom I am detaching only to aid you will soon be able to return. That would give me the highest satisfaction . . .

---

[35] *Loc. cit.*

[36] Duquesne to Marin, June 13, 1753, Archives du Séminaire de Québec, V-V, 5:62:5. The Governor was not criticizing him, for he added that he would gladly give him that rank if he could.

[37] Duquesne to the Minister, November 2, 1753, *Wilderness Chronicles,* 58-60. Jacques Legardeur, Sieur de Saint-Pierre (1701-1755), had been in command of trading posts in the vicinity of Lake Winnepeg, and had just returned to Canada.

I exhort you, Sir, to take care of your health, which gives me keen anxiety, and I hope with all my heart that joy will replace it from the return of your health which is so dear to me. . . .[38]

Despite Marin's illness, Duquesne understood that Péan was proceeding with the plans for the descent of the Ohio:

Sieur Péan also informs me that the last portage is finished, and that he is going to send on his bark canoes, in order to be ready to leave on the 10th or 12th of October, with 180 pirogues which were all ready to enter the Riviere d'Oyo.[39]

Again the illness among the troops was mentioned:

This officer informs me that his detachment will consist of only 900 men because of the scurvy which broke out among them. This is a reduction to 500 men less than I planned. . . .[40]

Still the Governor did not anticipate that Péan would have any difficulty in proceeding down the Ohio to the Illinois country with the eight hundred men which would be left after building and garrisoning a third fort at Chiningué.[41] He even spoke of the good fortune with which the transportation of men and supplies had been carried out, although he did say: "The dangerous condition of Sieur Marin, as well as such a large number of invalids, makes up for this in a way that I feel keenly, although the scurvy of these militia is seldom fatal."[42]

Other Canadian officials failed to share the Governor's optimism. As early as October 13, Bigot's deputy Varin wrote Contrecoeur, "I hope M. Péan will have the satisfaction of seeing the Illinois during December, but I greatly fear that the grave diseases which are attacking the army will make it impossible for him to carry out this errand."[43]

Sometime in October, Marin's health took a turn for the better, and he began again to look to the south. He sent Drouillon to inspect the Rivière aux Boeufs, and was dismayed to receive yet another report that the stream was too low to float the loaded pirogues. To make doubly certain, he sent out two other officers, Carqueville and Portneuf, who made the same report: the Rivière aux Boeufs could not serve as a waterway for the expedition that fall.[44]

---

[38] Duquesne to Marin, October 14, 1753, *Papiers Contrecoeur*, 74.

[39] Duquesne to the Minister, November 2, 1753, *Wilderness Chronicles*, 58-60.

[40] *Ibid.*

[41] *Ibid.* The original plan was to build the third fort, Fort Duquesne, at Chiningué (Logstown).

[42] Duquesne to the Minister, November 2, 1753, *Wilderness Chronicles*, 58-60.

[43] Varin to Contrecoeur, October 13, 1753, *Papiers Contrecoeur*, 72-73.

[44] Severance, *An Old Frontier of France*, II, 20-21, apparently based on the *Mémoire pour Michel-Jean-Hugues Péan*.

Other exasperating disappointments tormented the ailing commander. According to Stephen Coffin, Marin hired a hundred Loup Indians to carry supplies on horseback to the Belle Rivière, presumably to Joncaire's post at Venango. "They set off with full Loads, but never deliver'd them to the French, which incensed them very much, being not only a loss, but a great disappointment."[45]

A similar instance of Indian thievery was described by Marin in an angry letter:

> I am writing you, my dear friend, this letter full of wrath about our portage. The Indians have carried off our blankets, and especially the white ones—big, middle-sized, and small—so that I do not have any left to supply the posts. That is why I beg you, my dear friend, to take any steps to get plenty of white blankets, big, middle-sized, and small . . ."[46]

These successive disappointments made the sick old commander even more conscious of the impending failure of his campaign and drove him to desperation, if the account of Stephen Coffin may be believed. According to the English deserter,

> Morang a man of very Peevish Cholerick disposition meeting with those and other crosses, and finding the Season of the Year too far advanced to build the third Fort, called all his Officers together, and told them, that as he had Engaged and firmly promised the Governor to finish the three Forts that Season, and not being able to fulfill the same, was both Afraid and Ashamed to return to Canada being sencible he had now forfited the Governors favour forever; wherefore rather than live in disgrace he begged the would take him; as he then sat in a Carriage made for him, being very sick some time, and seat him in the Middle of the Fort, and then set fire to it, and Lett him perish in the [Flames.][47]

Naturally enough, the officers declined to carry out such a delirious suggestion. Coffin's story of this incident is made the more convincing by his naive explanation of their refusal, that the officers "[had not the least Regard for him,] as he had behaved very ill to them [all in] general."[48]

Marin's subordinate officers must have been perplexed and disturbed about the hazardous situation of the army, isolated in the wilderness, with sickness increasing throughout the camps, and with a commander

---

[45] Examination of Stephen Coffin, January 10, 1754, Sir William Johnson Manuscripts, Vol. 23, p. 170. New York State Library.

[46] Letter from Marin, undated, Archives du Séminaire de Québec, V-V, 5:60:11. Marin went on to remark, "The rains are going to be frequent in the season we are entering."

[47] Examination of Stephen Coffin, January 10, 1754, loc. cit.

[48] Ibid. The words in brackets are supplied from the version in Wilderness Chronicles, 47.

incapacitated by illness. At a distance, their efforts to put things right looked like insubordination. On November 7, Duquesne wrote Marin promising him justice "for the most insubordinate action of M. de Repentigni,"[49] the commander of Fort Presque Isle. On November 29, the Governor told the Minister,

> I have put a stop to the letters of Sieur de Repentigny, Captain, who was insubordinate to Sieur Marin, his commander, in letting me know secretly of the slackness of the detachment; but as he wrote to me alone to give the first news of it and as I see clearly it is only because of an indiscreet zeal, the usual thing in the service of this country, I intend for the sake of an example to punish him by imprisonment on his return, for he is otherwise a very good man.[50]

The Governor's remarks tend to support another story related by Stephen Coffin about Marin's last days, that a special messenger, "Chevalier Le Crake,"[51] came from Canada "in a birch Canoe, worked by 10 men," to bring Marin "a Cross of Saint Lewis, which the Rest of the Officers would not allow him to take, unless the Governor was Acquainted of his Conduct and Behaviour."[52] On September 10, Governor Duquesne did write Marin that he was sending "a canoe for the express purpose of bringing to you the Cross of St. Louis which the King has sent for you," and gave him permission to wear it at once without waiting for his formal admission to the order.[53] It does not seem entirely unlikely that the officers might have acted in this way, and it is difficult to see how such a story could have been imagined by Coffin.[54] Yet, on October 7, Joncaire at Venango sent Marin his "sincere compliments" on his new rank, and said, "I hope I shall have similar satisfaction in hearing of the perfect recovery of your health."[55] It is conceivable that the Indian agent would not know what had happened at Fort Le Boeuf, and that his news of Marin's advancement came direct from Canada.[56]

Stephen Coffin's account of the unhappy situation of the French commander may be untrustworthy as to detail, but the general picture

---

[49] Duquesne to Marin, November 7, 1753, *Papiers Contrecoeur*, 78-79.

[50] Duquesne to the Minister, November 29, 1753, *Wilderness Chronicles*, 60-62.

[51] Not identified.

[52] Examination of Stephen Coffin, January 10, 1754, *loc. cit.*

[53] Duquesne to Marin, September 10, 1753, *Papiers Contrecoeur*, 64.

[54] It is conceivable that the officers objected to Marin receiving the decoration, not particularly because of "his Conduct and Behaviour," but because the campaign was failing—or even because he was too ill.

[55] Joncaire to Marin, October 7, 1753, *Papiers Contrecoeur*, 69-70.

[56] Joncaire received letters from the Governor; Joncaire to Marin, August 16, 1753, Archives du Séminaire de Québec, V-V, 5:60:1, mentions such a letter.

of Marin's distress and misery, of his feeling of disgrace and failure, and of the officers' attitude toward him, is not unconvincing. It was impossible for the expedition to descend to the Ohio that fall, impossible to consider building the third fort, and impossible to send on Péan and his detachment to winter in the Illinois country. The dying commander, who had begun his campaign in the spring with such high hopes, must have felt his failure keenly.

Circumstances compelled a decision to halt the campaign for that year. Of the more than two thousand men who had left Montreal in the spring and summer, there remained only eight hundred fit for continued service.[57] Marin decided, or was persuaded, to send Péan and Le Mercier back to Montreal with all the troops, except what were needed to garrison the forts and begin preparations for another campaign the next year. For the Governor, Marin prepared a detailed report, giving the drought as the chief reason for not advancing to the Belle Rivière, and appending a statement signed by Drouillon, Carqueville, and Portneuf, the officers who had examined the Rivière aux Boeufs.[58] But though Péan and most of the army departed, Marin himself remained at Fort Le Boeuf. In Duquesne's words, "he preferred to die on the field of battle rather than return home to regain his health."[59] Not long after his army left for home, the old commander died, on October 29, 1753, leaving the command temporarily in the hands of Repentigny, of whose insubordination he had had occasion to complain.

In the words of the burial record, "His remains were interred in the cemetery of the same fort and during the campaign of the Belle Rivière. There were present at his interment Monsieur Repentigny, commander of the above-mentioned army and captain of infantry; Messieurs du Muys, lieutenant of infantry; Benois, lieutenant of infantry; de Simblim,[60] major at the above-mentioned fort; La Force, keeper of the stores, who have signed with us." With their signatures is the name of the Recollect priest and chaplain, Father Denys Baron.[61]

Ten days before the death of the French commander, the Indians at Venango gave Joncaire a message to send him. They condoled with

---

[57] *Mémoire pour Michel-Jean-Hugues Péan*, 62, cited in Frégault, *Bigot*, II, 67.

[58] Severance, *An Old Frontier of France*, II, 21.

[59] Duquesne to the Minister, October 7, 1754, *Wilderness Chronicles*, 63.

[60] Duverger de Saint-Blin, who was to command at Fort Le Boeuf from 1755 to 1759.

[61] Severance, *An Old Frontier of France*, II, 23-24, translating *Registres des baptésmes et sepultures qui se sont faits au Fort Duquesne pendant les années 1753, 1754, 1755 & 1756*. The translation has been slightly modified, changing Beautiful River back to Belle Rivière.

Marin on the death of so many of his men, and expressed disappointment at his delay in coming down the river. Their poetic phrases may serve as valedictory to the ill-fated expedition of 1753:

My father, we do not doubt at all the sorrow you must feel at not being able to go among your children to comfort them.

The Master of Life disposes of us all. He calls, whenever He wishes, those whom He has placed on earth. With these strings we wipe your tears which you shed for the loss of your warriors whom you are losing continually. We cleanse your body covered with their blood. It is the Master of Life who takes them from you. Let us follow His will.

Think, my father, continually of the good things for which you were sent, and of which we are convinced.

We give you, my father, a sweet medicine which will cast off all the grief you have for the loss of your warriors. It is not only you who lose them. We, too, grieve for them. It is in the name of the Loups and in our own name[62] that we bring you this speech.[63]

These Indians made it plain that the failure of the French to descend the river would mean hardship to them, too.

My father, for a long time you have promised to come and comfort us, and take care of us and our children.

We fear that the drought may prevent your coming down. Be mindful, my father, that you have driven off all the English, and that your children will be in a pitiable state if they do not see you here. Or, should you wish them to stretch out their necessities, the winter is long. Even the children are waiting for you with pleasure. Remember your promise and remember them; do not abandon them.[64]

The coming of the French had disrupted the trade the Indians of Venango had carried on with the English, and left them dependent on the French. The death of Marin and the return of his army to Canada left these Indians without hope of getting supplies for the winter. By February, 1754, Joncaire was to write of their desperate condition and of their constant begging:

. . . I even believe that they have boiled the casks to smell the odor. Sometimes it is a sick man who sends to ask for a piece of bread, sometimes for a drink of wine. One is going to die, another cannot go hunting for lack of gunpowder. One has neither a shirt nor leggings; another's dead parents torment him continually in his sleep, reproaching him for not taking pity on them and for not feasting them with brandy; finally the devil sends others to ask for blankets, recalling all the promises made to them last summer, at

---

[62] These "residents [domiciliers] of the Rivierre au Boeuf" describe themselves as "men of the Five Nations"—that is, Iroquois.

[63] Joncaire to Marin, October 19, 1753, *Papiers Contrecoeur*, 76-77.

[64] *Ibid.*

the same time taking great pains to have it understood that, when the English were there, they did not suffer so much.[65]

But the disappointment of these Indians was no greater than Governor Duquesne's chagrin when he learned that the troops were returning with only part of their mission accomplished. He made the best of things, however, and wrote Marin[66] kindly on November 7, "Everything will be all right, Sir, if your good constitution restores itself. I was dismayed to learn M. Lemercier's decision [to return], but I was not, and am not, overcome by it as long as you are still around." Far from reproaching him for failure, Duquesne said he was reporting to the Minister that, "on this occasion, you have crowned the work with prudence." Praising his "wise decision," the Governor looked to the future: "It is up to me to procure what you need and a whole fresh troop. That is what I shall work on when I am in Montreal, where I am going to spend the winter." He concluded with the news that the Court had ordered that "the forts of Anjou,[67] Sonioto,[68] and Sandosqués"[69] should not be built, so that the only fort on the Belle Rivière would be "Fort de Chinengué."[70]

On November 16, Duquesne wrote to Marin again, for he was still unaware of his death. In fact, he still had hope of Marin's recovery, for Péan told him, "He had received one of your letters in which you tell him that you were better and that you were sleeping." The Governor spoke sympathetically of the condition of the returning troops: "Since I have been constantly extolling your care and foresight in sending these exhausted men back to me, instead of leaving them exposed to die along the road they were to take, or bringing disgrace to the King's arms if any rogues had attacked this troop which was so worn out as to be totally unrecognizable." He repeated that he was working on "all the necessary arrangements" so that Marin

---

[65] Joncaire to Saint-Pierre, February 20, 1754, *Papiers Contrecoeur*, 101-103.

[66] News of Marin's death did not reach Canada until some time after the return of Péan and Le Mercier, and the Governor wrote several more letters to him.

[67] The name Anjou seems not to have been actually used for any place on the Belle Rivière, but on one or two French maps it is used for Venango, the Indian village and trading post at the mouth of French Creek. However, it may possibly refer to Paille Coupée ("cut straw") which the French had originally planned to fortify; see Bigot to the Minister, October 26, 1752, *Wilderness Chronicles*, 41. It may be a mere coincidence that Anjou's historic symbol was the broomstraw (*planta genesta*, whence the name Plantagenet for the Angevin dynasty in England), but it is at least worth noting.

[68] The Scioto River, in Ohio.

[69] Sandusky, on Lake Erie.

[70] Duquesne to Marin, November 7, 1753, *Papiers Contrecoeur*, 78-79.

could "begin again better and earlier than ever," and told him to continue the preparations for the next spring's campaign. He even reminded him, in a postscript, to have the men "sow corn and peas."[71]

In his report to the Minister on November 29, the Governor placed even more emphasis on the distressing condition of the returning soldiers, and on Marin's wisdom in giving up the campaign that fall:

> I have myself reviewed the detachment which has returned from the Riviere au Boeuf, and I could not help being touched by the pitiable state to which it has been reduced by the excessive labor of the portages and sleeping in the open for almost three months.
> There is no reason to doubt that if these weakened men had set out to reach their destination, the Riviere d'Oyo would have been strewn with dead men, because of the fevers and lung diseases which were beginning to attack this troop, and because ill-disposed Indians would not have failed to attack them when they were nothing but spectres.

From "the wise course taken by Sieur Marin" the Governor foresaw these results: "the sparing of a large number of inhabitants for the colony"; the saving of "the provisions already brought to the last storehouse"; and eliminating the expense of feeding "this troop during its wintering with the Illinois." He added, "There is more reason to hope for complete success, if a selected and completely fresh troop, which has suffered no hardship, is sent out to take up the campaign. . . ."[72]

Still later, in writing to Marin's successor, Legardeur de Saint-Pierre, the Governor said that the "only reproach" he could make about Marin was that he had felt it necessary "to use the lack of water in the Riviere au Boeuf as an excuse for resting his detachment." The excuse itself was suspicious, the Governor implied: "If I myself had not reviewed the militia, whom I found exhausted to the point that some are dying every day, I would never have been able to keep myself from being suspicious about this maneuver which crowned the wisdom of this commander. . . . And I was very certain that he could not enter the Belle Riviere with such cadavers who undoubtedly would have imperilled the King's arms."[73]

The following year, the government in Paris asked questions about the halting of the expedition with its task incomplete, and Governor Duquesne made his final summation of the causes of failure. He was inclined to discount the drought and the low water in the streams, and said that Marin "could not be blamed for not having soundings

---

[71] Duquesne to Marin, November 16, 1753, *Papiers Contrecoeur*, 81.
[72] Duquesne to the Minister, November 29, 1753, *Wilderness Chronicles*, 60-61.
[73] Duquesne to Saint-Pierre, December 25, 1753, *Papiers Contrecoeur*, 87-88.

made of the Riviere au Boeuf which he was to go down, because all these little rivers of the south, including those of Tchatakoin, dry up during the summer when there is no rain. A twenty-four hours' storm makes them navigable to such an extent that, a week after the departure homeward of the detachment, loaded pirogues descended this same Riviere au Boeuf, and this year it was navigated all summer, for it rained frequently."[74] Here the Governor was undoubtedly defending his own decision to change the route of the expedition from the Chautauqua portage to Presque Isle.

Duquesne thought the real cause was quite evident:

There was only one reason, the number of invalids who must be brought back to Montreal, which made him decide on this departure, as he would not have had a sufficient force left to enter the Belle Riviere, especially since the Sonont8ans[75] had mutinied and insolently blocked the road. I regard this move as the most prudent one that Sieur Marin has made.[76]

In other words, the sickness among the troops had reduced their effectiveness to the point that the hostility of the Half King and his Indians had to be reckoned as a real danger. To this extent, the Half King's speech at the Council of Presque Isle on September 3 did succeed in halting the French.

---

[74] Duquesne to the Minister, October 7, 1754, *Wilderness Chronicles,* 63.

[75] The French name for the Senecas, here applied generally to the Ohio Iroquois whom the English called Mingoes.

[76] Duquesne to the Minister, October 7, 1754, *Wilderness Chronicles,* 63.

Young Washington delivers Governor Dinwiddie's letter.
—an artist's sketch from the statue at the Fort Le Boeuf Memorial in Waterford.

WASHINGTON VISITS FORT LE BOEUF

In the first year's campaign, the French forces had been able to carry out only a part of Governor Duquesne's plan. Instead of the entire Ohio country, only the gateway of the Presque Isle Portage was securely in their hands, with Fort Le Boeuf and Fort Presque Isle guarding each end of the military road. The rest of the Ohio country was still to be occupied. To be sure, there were French traders at Logstown, and Captain Joncaire was stationed at Venango with a small detachment; but these served only to gather information about English activities and to influence the Indians, preparing the way for actual seizure of the country. Disease, drought, and the threat of Indian hostility had delayed by more than half a year the schedule of operations outlined in October, 1752.[1] The British and their colonies of Virginia and Pennsylvania had thus been granted additional time in which to act against the French invasion. If the British had been able

---

[1] Bigot to the Minister, October 26, 1752, *Wilderness Chronicles*, 39-43. The passage in question is quoted above on page 14.

to act with vigor and decision, sending an effective force to hold a key point like the Forks of the Ohio, the French might not have proceeded farther with their occupation of the Belle Rivière.[2]

The French had been counting on the slowness of the British colonies to take action. In June, 1753, Governor Duquesne had contemptuously dismissed a rumor that an English army of six thousand men was being raised to send to the Ohio: "That is a good thing to tell Indians, who do not know that to raise an English troop more time and threats are necessary than for levying Canadians."[3] Duquesne seemed to assume that British action would be too little and too late, and his assumption was correct.

Not until the end of October did a British governor act at all, and then it was only by sending a message to warn the French that they were trespassing on British territory, and to order them to withdraw peaceably. Governor Dinwiddie of Virginia, whose instructions required him to issue such a warning before using armed force to drive out the intruders, attempted to arrange for a joint protest through Governor Hamilton of Pennsylvania and Governor Clinton of New York, but without success.[4] Then he decided to act alone. On October 31, 1753, two days after Marin's death, Governor Dinwiddie commissioned a young man of twenty-one, member of a leading Virginia family, "to visit and deliver a letter to the Commandant of the *French* forces on the *Ohio*." Thus George Washington entered upon his first important public service, setting out from Williamsburg "on the intended Journey the same day."[5]

Consequently, on December 4, Captain Philippe Thomas de Joncaire[6] received visitors at his post at Venango, in John Fraser's former trading establishment. After a long and arduous journey, young

---

[2] The French forces on the Ohio were never very large. In 1753 Marin had little more than 2,000 men, and his effective force was much smaller than that. In 1754 Governor Duquesne planned to have Contrecoeur descend the Allegheny with only 600 men; see Duquesne to Contrecoeur, January 27, 1754, *Papiers Contrecoeur*, 93.

[3] Duquesne to Marin, June 13, 1753, Archives du Séminaire de Québec, V-V, 5:62:5.

[4] Lawrence H. Gipson, *Zones of International Friction*, 294-296, gives details about Dinwiddie's instructions and about his dealings with the other governors.

[5] Fitzpatrick, ed., *The Diaries of George Washington*, I, 43.

[6] As has been indicated earlier, the elder of the Joncaire brothers had been on the Ohio since 1750, first at Chiningué, then at Paille Coupée, and finally at Venango, where he arrived on August 28, 1753. There are letters indicating that he remained there during the winter of 1753-1754. However, Severance, *An Old Frontier of France*, II, 34-35, thinks that it was the younger brother, Joncaire de Chabert, who received Washington. This is his evidence: At his trial in Paris, along with Bigot, Péan, and the others, Chabert presented a *mémoire* relating, among other

Washington arrived there with an oddly-assorted escort. Christopher Gist, his guide; the Dutchman Jacob Van Braam, his French interpreter; John Davison, his Indian interpreter; and three other frontiersmen made up the white contingent, and at Logstown four Indians had joined the party: the Half King, two other leaders of the Ohio Indians, and a young hunter, who was later the famous Guyasutha (Kiashuta).[7] The Virginian emissary had traveled through the wilderness, delayed by "the excessive Rains and vast Quantity of Snow,"[8] and by conferences with the Indians at Logstown. On the way he had taken every opportunity to gather information about the country and about the doings of the French. At Fraser's new trading post at Turtle Creek on the Monongahela, he had learned of Marin's death and of "the Return of the major Part of the *French* Army into Winter Quarters." Passing by the Forks of the Ohio, he had noted that the Point was "extremely well situated for a Fort,"[9] and at Logstown he had begun to get many details about French operations and intentions.

From French deserters at Logstown, Washington knew that the invaders had fallen short of carrying out their entire program for the year 1753. These Frenchmen had been sent from Louisiana to the Illinois[10] country with provisions, presumably to supply Péan's detachment when it came down the Ohio to winter there. When the detachment failed to arrive, these men had deserted. From the Half King, Washington had a detailed account of the Council at Presque Isle in September, when the Indian leader had asked the French not to invade his country. The Half King had also told him about the two forts the French had built, "one on Lake *Erie,* and another on

---

services, that he was sent to the Ohio and to the Iroquois during the winter of 1753-1754. But since this errand to the Indians was "to notify them, in the Governor's name, that he was going to the Ohio to take possession of it, and to build forts on its banks," it obviously belongs to the previous winter of 1752-1753. But Varin grumbled in a letter to Contrecoeur, September 8, 1752, that Chabert would not even winter at his post of Little Fort Niagara because "his lady is here [in Montreal], and a hair of some one you love draws more than four oxen." (*Papiers Contrecoeur,* 11.) And in 1753 Duquesne sent Chabert permission to return to Montreal for the winter (Duquesne to Contrecoeur, July 10, 1753, Archives du Séminaire de Québec, V-V, 1:23). The probability is that Chabert, in preparing his defence, took over, and adopted as his own, assignments which were actually carried out by his older brother. After all, it was a family affair!

[7] Fitzpatrick, ed., *Diaries,* I, 43, 46, 54. The "Hunter" is known to have been Guyasutha because Washington met him on the Ohio in 1770 and identified him as "one of the Indians that went with me to the French in 1753." *Diaries* I, 423.

[8] *Ibid.,* I, 44.

[9] *Ibid.*

[10] Understanding this as "îles noires," Van Braam translated it "Black Islands."

French-Creek near a small Lake about 15 Miles asunder and a large Waggon Road between." The old Iroquois had even described the forts and drawn a plan for Washington.[11]

The Virginian officer had already observed the workings of French "forest diplomacy," and knew how the Indians were wavering between neutrality and resistance. He knew that Joncaire had recently called together *"Mingo's, Delawares,*[12] &c.*"* at Venango and warned them "not to intermeddle" with the French plans to seize the Belle Rivière. Joncaire had been reported as saying,

> that they intended to have been down the River this Fall, but the Waters were growing cold, and the Winter advancing, which obliged them to go into Quarters: But that they might assuredly expect them in the Spring, with a far greater Number. . . . That though they had lost their General, and some few of their Soldiers, yet there were Men enough to reinforce them, and make them masters of the *Ohio*.[13]

Washington was, therefore, already well informed about the doings of the French, when he reached the post of "Captain *Joncaire,* their Interpreter in Chief . . ., and a Man of Note in the Army," as well as "a Person of great great Influence among the *Indians*."[14] The young officer found the French flag flying "at a House from which they had driven Mr. *John Frazier*," and went there to meet Joncaire, who told him "that he had the command of the *Ohio*; But that there was a General Officer at the near Fort," to whom the letter from Governor Dinwiddie should be taken.[15] The "Man of Note" gave a gracious and agreeable reception to the "Person of Distinction," as Dinwiddie had recently described his emissary in a letter to Governor Hamilton of Pennsylvania.[16] In Washington's words, "He invited us to sup with them; and treated us with the greatest Complaisance." But in the course of the evening's conversation, "The Wine, as they dosed themselves pretty plentifully with it, . . . gave a licence to the Tongues to reveal their Sentiments more freely." Joncaire and his fellow officers admitted, "That it was their absolute Design to take Possession of the *Ohio*, and by G—— they would do it; For that altho' they were sensible the *English* could raise two Men for their one; yet they knew their Motions were too slow and dilatory to prevent any Undertaking of

[11] Fitzpatrick, ed., *Diaries*, I, 46, 47-49.

[12] The French would have said "Iroquois" (or "Sonontouans") and "Loups."

[13] Fitzpatrick, ed., *Diaries*, I, 52-53.

[14] *Ibid.*, I, 53, 56.

[15] *Ibid.*, I, 54-55.

[16] Dinwiddie to Hamilton, November 24, 1753, *Colonial Records*, V, 712.

theirs." Washington even picked up details about the size of the French forces, the location of their forts, the withdrawal of troops to winter quarters, and the length of the trip from Montreal.[17]

The following day, December 5, it rained so heavily that Washington could not leave for Fort Le Boeuf. A further cause of delay was that his Indian companions wanted to talk to Joncaire. They wanted to return the "French Speech-Belts" as a sign that they rejected the French notice, and would not promise to be passive bystanders when their country was invaded. The clever Joncaire knew how to handle Indians, however, for he "made several trifling Presents; and applied Liquor so fast, that they were soon rendered incapable of the Business they came about, notwithstanding the Caution which was given." Next morning, the Half King had sobered up, and still wanted to deliver the belt to Joncaire. Washington tried to persuade him to wait and give it to the commander at Fort Le Boeuf, but the Half King explained that Venango was the place where the "Council Fire was kindled, where all their Business with these People was to be transacted." But when the Council assembled, and when the Indian leader "spoke much the same as he had before done to [Marin]," Joncaire temporized. He declined to accept the "Speech-Belt," and told the Half King to take it "to the Fort to the Commander."[18]

On December 7, there was further delay, as the Half King had a bone to pick with Custaloga, the Delaware chief at Venango. He had brought orders from "King Shingiss," the Delaware chief near the Forks of the Ohio, that Custaloga should deliver up the French belt given to the Delawares. But this chief, living at Venango under the eyes of the French, refused to cooperate.[19] Finally, at eleven o'clock, Washington set out from Venango, now with four Frenchmen added to his escort. Because of "excessive Rains, Snows, and bad Travelling, through many Mires and Swamps," the party did not reach Fort Le Boeuf until December 11.[20]

Here Washington was again received with courtesy. After a night's rest, he was presented to Legardeur de Saint-Pierre, who had arrived

---

[17] *Ibid.*, I, 55-56. Washington even reported that "From the Fort on Lake *Erie* to *Montreal* is about 600 Miles, which they say requires no more, of [during] good Weather, than four Weeks Voyage, if they go in Barks or large Vessels, so that they may cross the Lake: But if they come in Canoes it will require 5 or 6 Weeks, for they are obliged to keep under the Shore." This information tallies very well with the time taken by Céloron's expedition and by Marin's various detachments.

[18] Fitzpatrick, ed., *Diaries*, I, 56-57.

[19] *Ibid.*, I, 54, 57.

[20] *Ibid.*, I, 58.

on December 3 to replace the dead commander.[21] Washington described the French officer as "an elderly Gentleman" with "much the air of a Soldier."[22] The young Virginian was impressed by the distinguished bearing of his host, but he probably never knew that Saint-Pierre was the last of New France's explorers of the Far West—that he had just returned from an expedition as far as Lake Winnipeg and almost to the Rockies.

Washington explained his business, and offered the letter from the Governor of Virginia, but the commander asked him to keep it until the arrival of Legardeur de Repentigny, the commander at Fort Presque Isle, who had been sent for because he "understood a little *English*." Repentigny arrived at one o'clock, Washington finally delivered the letter, and then the two French officers went into another room to translate it. Afterward, at Saint-Pierre's invitation, Washington and his interpreter read and verified the French version.[23]

The Governor of Virginia had phrased his summons to the French in the following terms:

> The lands upon the River Ohio, in the western parts of the Colony of Virginia, are so notoriously known to be the property of the Crown of Great Britain that it is a matter of equal concern and surprise to me, to hear that a body of French forces are erecting fortresses and making settlements upon that river, within His Majesty's dominions.

>   *   *   *   *

> . . . It becomes my duty to require your peaceable departure; and that you would forbear prosecuting a purpose so interruptive of the harmony and good understanding, which His Majesty is desirous to continue and cultivate with the most Christian King.[24]

The next day, December 13, the French officers held a council of war to decide what to do about Dinwiddie's letter, and Washington

---

[21] Washington says that Saint-Pierre "arrived here about seven Days before me." He was only one day off; see Duquesne to Saint-Pierre, December 25, 1753, *Papiers Contrecoeur,* 87-88.

[22] Fitzpatrick, ed., *Diaries,* I, 58. Actually, Saint-Pierre was 52 years old, but the hardships of the trip from the Far West to Montreal, and then to Fort Le Boeuf, may well have made him look elderly. Indeed, his health had given way, and he had asked for recall, which was granted in the letter cited in the preceding note.

[23] Fitzpatrick, ed., *Diaries,* I, 58-59.

[24] Dinwiddie to Saint-Pierre, October 31, 1753, *Wilderness Chronicles,* 76-77; also in O'Callaghan, ed., *Documents Relative to the Colonial History of the State of New York,* X, 258; *Pennsylvania Archives,* Second Series, VI, 174; Freeman, *Washington,* I, 309-310 (from Sparks Transcripts, Virginia State Library) ; and so on. But these all appear to be back-translations from Repentigny's French version, as given in *Papiers Contrecoeur,* 77-78; and Margry, *Découvertes et établissements des Français* . . ., VI, 728-729.

took advantage of the opportunity to look around· and prepare a description of the fort. He even had his men "take an exact Account of the Canoes which were hauled-up to convey their Forces down in the Spring. This they did, and told 50 of Birch Bark, and 170 of Pine; besides many others which were blocked-out, in Readiness to make."[25] Washington's men must have had to roam the woods to count canoes, for the boatyards were some distance above and below the fort. Their count seems to have been accurate, for Duquesne had reported that, early in the fall, "180 pirogues . . . were all ready to enter the Riviere d'Oyo."[26]

At Fort Le Boeuf, as at Venango, Washington had to contend with "many Plots concerted to retard the Indians Business, and prevent their returning." Although Saint-Pierre received the Indians "privately," the Half King immediately told Washington "that he offer'd the Wampum to the Commander, who evaded taking it, and made many fair Promises of Love and Friendship." As evidence of his desire for peaceful trade, the French commander said "he would send some Goods down immediately to the *Logg*'s Town for them." Washington thought that their real purpose was to capture English traders, for he had heard that an officer was to head this party.[27] Not long afterward, a small detachment commanded by La Chauvignerie did descend the river to set up a French post at Logstown in preparation for the coming of the main force.[28] Again, Washington's information was correct.

It was not until the evening of the 14th that the French commander gave Washington his reply to Governor Dinwiddie's letter.[29] Saint-Pierre's answer to the British summons was polite but firm; he was unwavering in his resolve to carry out his Governor's orders:

Sir:

As I have the honor of commanding here in chief, Mr. Washington delivered me the letter which you wrote to the commander of the French troops.

I should have been glad if you had given him orders, or he had been inclined, to proceed to Canada to see our General, to whom it

[25] Fitzpatrick, ed., *Diaries*, I, 59.

[26] Duquesne to the Minister, November 2, 1753, *Wilderness Chronicles*, 59, summarizing Péan's letter of September 29.

[27] Fitzpatrick, ed., *Diaries*, I, 60.

[28] See the various letters from La Chauvignerie, Joncaire, and Saint-Blin to Saint-Pierre or Contrecoeur from February 10 to March 11, 1754, in *Papiers Contrecoeur*, 99-110. La Chauvignerie reached Chiningué (Logstown) on January 16.

[29] Fitzpatrick, ed., *Diaries*, I, 61. Saint-Pierre's letter was apparently dated December 15 (the "5" is blurred and could conceivably be a "3"), but clerical errors are not at all uncommon in the dating of letters.

belongs, rather than to me, to set forth the evidence and the reality of the rights of the King, my master, to the lands situated along the Belle Riviere, and to contest the pretensions of the King of Great Britain thereto.

I am going to send your letter to the Marquis Duquesne. His reply will be a law to me, and, if he should order me to communicate it to you, Sir, I can assure you that I shall neglect nothing to have it reach you very promptly.

As to the summons you send me to retire, I do not think myself obliged to obey it. Whatever may be your instructions, I am here by virtue of the orders of my General, and I entreat you, Sir, not to doubt for a moment that I have a firm resolution to follow them with all the exactness and determination which can be expected of the best officer.

I do not know that anything has happened in the course of this campaign which can be construed as an act of hostility, or as contrary to the treaties between the two Crowns; the continuation of which interests and pleases us as much as it does the English. If you had been pleased, Sir, to go into detail regarding the deeds which caused your complaints, I should have had the honor of answering you in the most positive manner, and I am sure that you would have had reason to be satisfied.

I have made it a particular duty to receive Mr. Washington with the distinction owing to your dignity, his position, and his own great merit. I trust that he will do me justice in that regard with you, and that he will make known to you the profound respect with which I am,

Sir,
Your most humble and most obedient servant,

LEGARDEUR DE ST. PIERRE

From the Fort of the Riviere au Beuf, December 15, 1753.[30]

Washington now had the letter of reply for Governor Dinwiddie, but he was unable to leave Fort Le Boeuf the next morning. Though the French commander treated him with the utmost surface courtesy, he was still "exerting every Artifice he could invent" to detain Washington's Indian companions. The young Virginian commented, "I can't say that ever in my Life I suffered so much Anxiety as I did in

---

[30] Translation adapted from that in *Wilderness Chronicles*, 77-78, using photographic facsimile of original in Freeman, *Washington*, I, between 343 and 344. Versions compared include Freeman, *op. cit.*, I, 325; O'Callaghan, ed., *Documents Relative to the Colonial History of the State of New York*, X, 259; *Pennsylvania Archives*, Second Series, VI, 175; and the following French versions: Margry, *op. cit.*, VI, 730-731; *Colonial Records*, V, 715-716; and *Papiers Contrecoeur*, 83-84. The last is apparently a copy made for Contrecoeur from Saint-Pierre's draft; it varies as to wording, and the paragraphs are in a different order. Oddly enough, it is dated December 16, probably the date when the copy was made.

this Affair: I saw that every Stratagem which the most fruitful Brain could invent, was practised, to win the Half-King to their Interest." Washington complained to Saint-Pierre that "keeping them, as they were Part of my Company, was detaining me." The veteran commander suavely brushed the complaint aside; he denied that he was detaining the Indians, feigning ignorance "of the Cause of their Stay." Washington soon discovered the cause, however: "He had promised them a present of Guns, &c, if they would wait 'till the morning." The young officer decided to wait, on the Indians' solemn promise "That nothing should hinder them in the Morning."[31]

The morning of the 16th came, and the French renewed their efforts to separate the Indians from the English. They gave the Half King and his companions the promised present, but "then endeavored to try the Power of Liquor." Washington had to remind the Half King insistently about his promise, before he would come away. After "a tedious and very fatiguing Passage" down French Creek, Washington reached Venango on December 22. There Joncaire was ready and waiting for the Indians, who finally yielded to the lure of French presents and liquor, and remained with the excuse that one of them "had hurt himself much." However, the Half King reassured Washington, telling him not to "be concerned, for he knew the French too well, for anything to engage him in their Behalf."[32] Certainly, Joncaire did fail to win him over, for the Half King was still on the British side a few months later, aiding Washington in the Fort Necessity campaign.

Washington left Venango on December 23, undoubtedly feeling relieved to get out of the area of French occupation safely. On the way back, however, he encountered the greatest hardships and perils of his trip, for most of the journey was made on foot with Gist as his sole companion. Fired upon by a hostile Indian, half-drowned in crossing the flooded Allegheny, facing icy winds and heavy snows, he called it "as fatiguing a Journey as it is possible to conceive," when he at last returned to Virginia. It was not until January 16, 1754, that he delivered the French commander's reply to the Governor in Williamsburg. He also gave the Governor the journal of his adventures, and was much surprised when Dinwiddie ordered it to be printed.[33] This straightforward, if unpolished, narrative—with its many details about French operations and intentions—made a strong

---

[31] Fitzpatrick, ed., *Diaries*, I, 61-62.

[32] *Ibid.*, I, 62-63.

[33] *Ibid.*, 41, 67.

impression in the British colonies and in Great Britain. Keen-minded, alert to observe, young Washington was the first qualified British witness to the French occupation, the first to give a trustworthy description. The correctness of his information and of his judgment was never in question, but it stands out even more strikingly two centuries later, in the light of the French sources. His journal, and the sketch map showing the country he traversed, helped to lift the

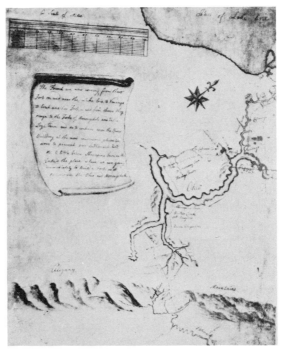

Washington's Map of the Ohio Country.
—*Public Archives of Canada.*

wilderness curtain obscuring the operations of the French in the Ohio country, at the end of the year 1753.[34]

To the French, Washington's mission and Governor Dinwiddie's letter were signs that the British were getting ready to oppose their seizure of the Ohio. On December 22, Legardeur de Saint-Pierre wrote to tell Governor Duquesne about this development. Duquesne thanked him on January 30, 1754, "for sending Sieur de Normanville

---

[34] The chief emphasis here has been on Washington's dealings with the French, and on what he found out from them. Details about his journey may be found in many other works.

express to inform me about the deputation from the Governor of Virginia, as well as for the care you took to send me the letter which he wrote to you." The Governor stated, "His claims on the Belle Riviere are sheer imagination, for it belongs to us incontestably. Moreover, the King wishes it, and that is enough for us to go forward. . . ."

The commander of Fort Le Boeuf must have hinted that Marin's instructions had given him no guidance in this case, for the Governor expressed surprise "that you did not find the instructions I gave the late M. Marin precise enough. You had them in your possession, however, for two whole days when I thought you would take his place for the operation in question; and you told me, when you returned them, that an officer would go ahead confidently with such a handsome proof of his General's trust."[35]

But Duquesne expressed himself more fully in his letters to Contrecoeur, the commander at Fort Niagara, whom he had already notified of his assignment to replace the ailing Saint-Pierre. On January 27, the Governor wrote, "I have no reason to suppose that either the English or the Indians have any desire to oppose by open force our taking possession of a location which belongs to us. . . ." Before this letter was sent, however, Duquesne received the news that the British had made official objections to the French occupation of the Ohio. He continued his letter on January 30, giving Contrecoeur instructions what to say and do in similar circumstances:

> Just as my letter was written, I received a dispatch from Sieur de Saint-Pierre who sent me express a letter from the Governor of Virginia in which he claims that the Belle Riviere belongs to them, and which summons the officer commanding the detachment to withdraw peaceably. Since this Governor does not write to me, I shall merely order you, in case he sends you another summons, to tell him your instructions state that the Belle Riviere and its dependencies belong incontestably to the Most Christian King; that as for insults contrary to international law, he can attribute none to us; and that if we stop the English who come to trade in our territory, it is because we have a right to do it, for we do not go on their land; that, moreover, the King my master asks only for his rights. He has no intention of disturbing the good harmony and friendship which prevail between His Majesty and the King of Great Britain.

To show his friendly attitude toward the British, the Governor cited the case of a little boy whom Canadian Indians had captured "in the direction of Carolina." He had forced the Indians to give up

---

[35] Duquesne to Saint-Pierre, January 30, 1754, *Papiers Contrecoeur*, 98-99.

the youngster, and had sent him back to Boston with a merchant. "In addition," the Governor continued, "he forbade all the Indians to exercise their usual cruelties against the English with whom we are friends." This was the line for Contrecoeur to follow: "There, Sir, are the replies you will make to this Governor, and even to others, in the event of a new deputation." But though the Marquis Duquesne apparently thought that Saint-Pierre could have been more explicit in his reply to Governor Dinwiddie, he was not critical, for he commented that it was "stamped with great dignity, firmness, and politeness."[36]

The British summons delivered at Fort Le Boeuf did give the Governor of New France some anxiety about the success of the expedition down the river in 1754, especially when he learned, on Saint-Pierre's return to Montreal, "about the unrest among the Indians and about the English gathering to build a fort." But on reflection he decided that it was impossible for them "to establish themselves solidly."[37] Washington's mission, therefore, had little immediate effect on the operations of the French, although it opened the way for eventual British action.

---

[36] Duquesne to Contrecoeur, January 27, 1754, continued January 30, *Papiers Contrecoeur,* 92-96.

[37] Duquesne to Contrecoeur, May 22, 1754, *Papiers Contrecoeur,* 128.

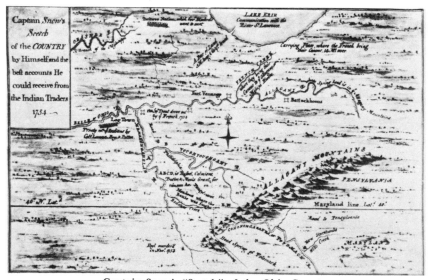

Captain Snow's "Scetch" of the Ohio Country.

—*Library of Congress.*

EPILOGUE

Shortly after Washington's visit to Fort Le Boeuf, Contrecoeur was transferred from Fort Niagara to lead a second expedition down to the Ohio in the spring of 1754. Thanks to the preparations made the previous year, this campaign went ahead on schedule, for the spring rains provided plenty of water in French Creek. By April 16, Contrecoeur reached the Forks of the Ohio, where a small detachment of Virginians had begun to erect a fort. By threat of force, the French compelled the Virginians to surrender, and then began to erect Fort Duquesne.

Daniel-Hyacinthe-Marie Lienard de Beaujeu. He commanded at Fort Niagara before Contrecoeur, and was to succeed him as commander of the Belle Rivière, but was killed in the Battle of the Monongahela.

—from "Pennsylvania Magazine of History and Biography."

The original plan had been to build Fort Duquesne at Logstown, further down the Ohio, but now it was felt that the Forks of the Ohio were a better location to halt English traders, and—perhaps—an English army. Another reason given was the lack of wood at Logstown. Apparently the Indians and the traders had used up all the trees for miles around, so that there was a shortage of logs at Logstown, and it would be difficult to build a fort there.

The English had moved to oppose the advance of the French, but their efforts were too little and too late. In April, while Contrecoeur was descending the Allegheny, Virginia troops under Washington were pressing toward the Forks of the Ohio, to come to the support of their new fort. But they were only part way when news came of its capture. Washington went forward even then, but hesitated when it appeared that the French might be too strong for him. While he was in this state of mind, the Half King brought him word that a French party was lurking nearby in a hidden place. Washington and his men, and the Half King and his Indians, marched through a rainy night to attack the French on the morning of May 28, 1754. The French leader, Jumonville, and several of his men were killed, and the rest were captured, except one who escaped at the beginning of the skirmish. This little engagement, which took place on the slope of Laurel Mountain in what is now Fayette County, was the first battle of the French and Indian War.

To take revenge, Contrecoeur sent out from Fort Duquesne a stronger force of French and Indians under Jumonville's brother, the Sieur de Villiers. Villiers came upon Washington entrenched in Fort Necessity, southeast of present Uniontown, and compelled him to surrender on July 4, 1754. In the articles of capitulation, Washington through ignorance of French unwittingly admitted that he had assassinated Jumonville. The French claimed that Jumonville had been an ambassador with a message warning the English to leave French territory—in other words, a message the opposite of what Washington had safely carried to Fort Le Boeuf a few months before. French propaganda later made good use of the admission into which Washington had been tricked.

In his departure from Fort Necessity, Washington's journal for this campaign fell into the hands of the French, and they used that in their propaganda, too. In fact, until recently, the only known version of Washington's journal for 1754 was a re-translation from a French version published in Paris in 1756, and there was considerable doubt as to its authenticity. In the Contrecoeur Papers, however, there is another and slightly different version which Governor Duquesne sent to Contrecoeur for his information and guidance. This version was not intended as propaganda, and its authenticity is much stronger.[1]

---

[1] For a fuller discussion and a translation of the newly-discovered version, see "Contrecoeur's Copy of George Washington's Journal for 1754," *Pennsylvania History*, January, 1952, reprinted as a pamphlet for the Pennsylvania Historical and Museum Commission.

Duquesne's irate comments on Washington and his journal confirm this: "There is nothing more unworthy, lower, or even blacker than the opinions and the way of thinking of this Washington! It would have been a pleasure to read his outrageous journal to him right under his nose."[2]

In 1755 the British made a stronger effort to drive the French from the Ohio country. Brigadier General Edward Braddock with an army of British regulars and provincial troops marched toward Fort Duquesne. Contrecoeur, and Beaujeu, who had just arrived at Fort Duquesne to replace the veteran commander, feared the worst, because their forces were inferior to the English. Contrecoeur remained in the fort, ready to destroy it and make a quick retreat, while Beaujeu and Dumas went out with 250 Frenchmen and 650 Indians to meet Braddock's army of 1450 men at the Turtle Creek crossing of the Monongahela, on July 9, 1755. Beaujeu was killed as the battle opened, at the third volley of the British; and this might well have demoralized the French. But Dumas rallied his forces, and by use of Indian methods of fighting completely routed the British. For days after the battle, the French had to work hard rounding up stray horses, and gathering up British cannon, guns, tools, and other ironwork from the battlefield. It was not only a glorious victory, it was a windfall!

With the victory over Braddock, the French invasion reached its climax, and the British colonies were now fully aware of the danger it meant to them. But years were to pass before the French could be dislodged from the Ohio country, as the superior strength of Britain and her colonies was eventually brought to bear. Not until 1758 were the French driven from Fort Duquesne by a British army under Brigadier General John Forbes; not until 1759 were they forced to evacuate their forts in northwestern Pennsylvania, after Sir William Johnson captured Fort Niagara. In the meantime, Indian war parties were sent out by the French to ravage the frontiers of Pennsylvania and other colonies, with such frightful effect that the conflict was called the French and Indian War. The war cry and the tomahawk brought fear and death into the peaceful Province of Pennsylvania which had not been touched by any of the earlier colonial wars.

---

[2] Duquesne to Contrecoeur, September 8, 1754, *Papiers Contrecoeur*, 251.

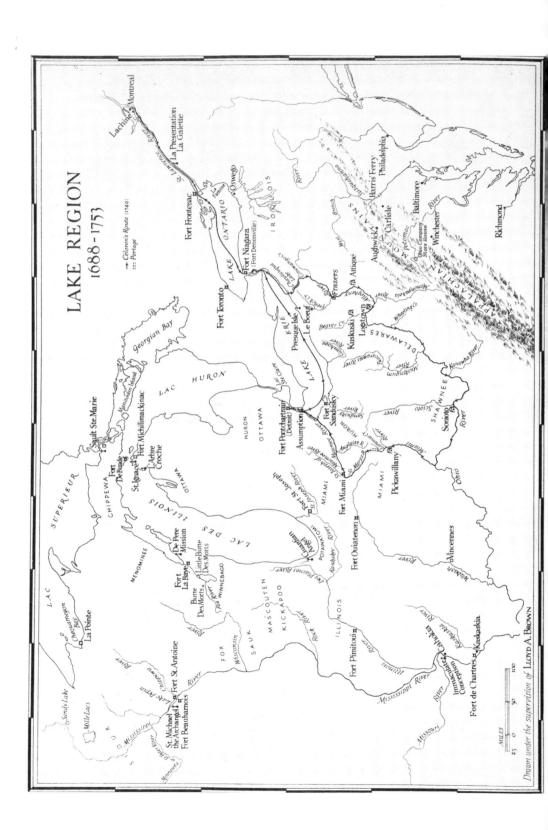

LAKE REGION
1688 – 1753

→ Céloron's Route (1749)
::: Portage

Richmond

Montreal
Lachine
La Presentation
La Galette
Oswego
Fort Frontenac
Fort Niagara (Fort Denonville)
Fort Toronto

Philadelphia
Harris's Ferry
Baltimore
Carlisle
Aughwick
Winchester
Ohio Company Store House

LAKE ONTARIO
La Famine
IROQUOIS

APPALACHIAN MOUNTAINS

Frazers
Attigué
Kuskuski
Logstown
DELAWARES

Potomac R.
Monongahela River
Wheeling Cr.
Beaver Cr.
Kanawha River

LAKE ERIE
Presque Isle
Le Boeuf
Chatauqua
French Cr.
Conewango
Allegheny R.

Georgian Bay

Manitoulin Island

LAC HURON

Ste Claire
Lac St Clair

Fort Pontchartrain (Detroit)
Assumption
Fort Sandusky

HURON
OTTAWA

Cayahoga River
Muskingum River
Kanawha River

Tuscarawas River
SHAWNEE
Muskingum River
Scioto River
Sonioto
River

Sault Ste. Marie
Fort De Buade
St. Ignace
L'Arbre Croche

LAC SUPERIEUR

CHIPPEWA

Chequamegon Bay
La Pointe

MENOMINEE

De Pere Mission
Fort La Baye
Little Butte Des Morts
Butte Des Morts
WINNEBAGO

OTTAWA
ILLINOIS

LAC DES ILLINOIS

POTAWATOMI
Chicagou
Angel

Fort St. Joseph
St. Joseph River
Kalamazoo River
Grand River
MIAMI
St. Marys River
Auglaize R.
Maumee River

Fort Miami
Pickawillany
MIAMI

Fort Ouiatenon
Fort Pimitoui
Wabash River
Vincennes

ILLINOIS
FOX
SAUK
MASCOUTEN
KICKAPOO

Fox River
Wisconsin River
Rock River
Des Plaines River

Mille Lacs
Sandy Lake
Lake Pepin
St. Michael the Archangel
Fort St. Antoine
Fort Beauharnois

Mississippi River
Chippewa River
St. Croix River
Minnesota River

Ohio

Immaculate Conception
Cahokia
Kaskaskia
Fort de Chartres
Kaskaskia River
Illinois River
Mississippi River
Missouri River

MILES
25 0   50   100

Drawn under the supervision of LLOYD A. BROWN

CHRONOLOGY

1752

July 30.	The Marquis Duquesne arrives in Quebec as Governor of New France.
October.	Duquesne and the Intendant Bigot complete plans for expedition to the Belle Rivière.
November 14.	Canadian militia levied for expedition.

1753

February 1.	Advance detachment commanded by Charles Deschamps de Boishébert leaves Montreal.
c. March 15.	Boishébert reaches Fort Niagara.
March 23.	Duquesne orders the landing to be made at Presque Isle, instead of Chatakoin.
c. April 15.	Boishébert lands at Chatakoin; explores Lake Erie shore as far as Presque Isle.
April 27.	Marin leaves La Chine with the main detachment.
c. May 3.	Boishébert's detachment lands at Presque Isle.
c. May 15.	The engineer Le Mercier reaches Presque Isle to supervise building of fort.
c. June 3.	Marin and the main detachment land at Presque Isle.
c. June 20.	Marin selects the site of Fort Le Boeuf.
July 12.	Marin begins Fort Le Boeuf.
August 14.	Conference of Marin, Péan, and Le Mercier at Presque Isle.
August 25.	Clearing of Rivière aux Boeufs begins.
August 28.	Joncaire arrives at Venango from Buckaloons.
Sept. 2-3.	Council of Presque Isle: the Half King warns Marin.
October 7.	Marin's illness reported to Duquesne.
October 14.	Duquesne assigns Legardeur de St. Pierre to aid Marin.
October 29.	Marin dies; Repentigny temporarily in command.
October 30.	Governor Dinwiddie writes to the French commandant.
November.	Le Mercier, Péan, and most of the troops return to Montreal.
December 3.	St. Pierre reaches Fort Le Boeuf.
December 5.	George Washington at Venango.
December 11-16.	Washington at Fort Le Boeuf.
December 25.	Duquesne recalls St. Pierre, and assigns Contrecoeur to command on Ohio.

1754

January 16.	Detachment under La Chauvignerie reaches Logstown (Chiningué).
January 30.	Duquesne gets news of Dinwiddie's letter.
February 10.	La Chauvignerie reports lack of wood at Logstown.
March 1.	Reinforcements reach Logstown.
March 6-7.	The French reconnoiter the Forks of the Ohio.
c. March 25.	Contrecoeur's expedition sets out from Fort Le Boeuf.
April 16.	Contrecoeur summons English to surrender their fort at the Forks of the Ohio.
May 23.	The Jumonville affair—Virginia force under Washington skirmishes with French party, killing or capturing all but one.
June 15.	Enclosure of Fort Duquesne completed.
June 28.	Coulon de Villiers sets out on campaign against Washington.
July 4.	Washington surrenders Fort Necessity.
July 24.	De Léry measures the Presque Isle portage.
September 8.	Duquesne receives translation of Washington journal.
October 30.	Duquesne notifies Contrecoeur that Beaujeu will relieve him in June, 1755.

1755

March 3.	Céloron's detachment leaves Montreal for the Ohio.
April 20.	Detachment leaves Montreal.
May 3, 5.	More detachments leave Montreal.
May 21.	Beaujeu's force begins to move from Niagara to Presque Isle.
June 1.	Contrecoeur hears of advance of British army under Braddock.
June 1.	Beaujeu at the end of the Niagara portage.
June 16.	Contrecoeur addresses Indian allies, Senecas, Cayugas, Shawnees, and Loups.
June 28.	Rigauville and 120 Hurons set out from Fort Duquesne to harass the English army.
July 8.	Council with the Indians to persuade them to join in attacking the English.
July 9.	Battle of the Monongahela. Beaujeu killed; Dumas wins the victory over Braddock.
July 12.	Huron allies leave for Detroit.
July 25.	Other Indians leave Fort Duquesne.
July 29.	Contrecoeur receives orders from Governor Vaudreuil to send out Indian war parties against the English frontier.
August 8.	Vaudreuil recalls Contrecoeur, and appoints Dumas to command in Ohio country.
November 15.	Contrecoeur leaves Fort Duquesne.

ACKNOWLEDGEMENTS

An important reason for the preparation of this pamphlet was the fact that a rich treasure of French sources has just become available, sources which have never before been used to any extent for this significant chapter of Pennsylvania history. These Contrecoeur Papers and related materials in the Archives du Séminaire de Québec have become accessible in a printed volume and on microfilm through a cooperative project of this important Canadian depository with the Institut d'histoire et de géographie de l'Université Laval, the Presses Universitaires Laval, and the Pennsylvania Historical and Museum Commission.

A special debt is owed to those who helped to make this material available: to Father Arthur Maheux and Father Honorius Provost, Archivist and Assistant Archivist of the Séminaire, who were its custodians; to Marius Barbeau, who listed the Papers for microfilming; to Professor Marcel Trudel, of the Université Laval, the chief adviser in the work of transcription and editing; and, last but not least, to Fernand Grenier, the editor of *Papiers Contrecoeur et autres documents concernant le conflit anglo-français sur l'Ohio de 1745 à 1756* (Quebec, Les Presses Universitaires Laval, 1952) : Monsieur Grenier's painstaking and accurate transcription of sources, his enlightening notes, and his excellent bibliography, have been indispensable aids in the preparation of this study. All the quotations derived from his book have been duly identified, but it would have been impossible to indicate all the places where his notes have been helpful.

The printed volume, it should be clearly understood, was never intended to be more than a selection of the more important sources. But the entire body of Contrecoeur Papers, Legardeur de Saint Pierre Papers, and Marin Papers in the Fonds Viger-Verreau of the Archives du Séminaire has been microfilmed by the Pennsylvania Historical and Museum Commission, which thus brought this great collection to Harrisburg. Reference to this material has been indicated by the designation, Archives du Séminaire de Québec, V-V.

The translations from the *Papiers Contrecoeur* were made by Dr. Armen Kalfayan and Miss Blair Hanson, of the faculty of Allegheny College, with my assistance. I have made the other translations, or taken them from printed collections of translated sources. As a special point, it should be noted that the French word "sauvage" has been uniformly rendered as "Indian," even in versions taken from printed translations.

Grateful acknowledgement is made to many persons who have read some or all of the manuscript and offered valuable suggestions. On the Commission staff they have included Dr. Paul A. W. Wallace, Research Consultant, and Editor of PENNSYLVANIA HISTORY; William A. Hunter, Senior Archivist, Public Records Division; Norman B. Wilkinson, Assistant State Historian; John Witthoft, Curator of Anthropology, Pennsylvania State Museum; and Mrs. Autumn Leonard, Research Assistant, who also helped to read the proof. I am also indebted to Merle H. Deardorff, of Warren, and Ross Pier Wright, of Erie, for reading the manuscript in the light of their knowledge and interest in this field, and offering advice and criticism.

Many other acknowledgements are also due. Charles Scribner's Sons gave gracious permission for the use of a map from the *Atlas of American History,* and the Buffalo Historical Society was generous in lending several cuts. Hon. William Kaye Lamb, Dominion Archivist, Public Archives of Canada, supplied copies of several portraits. Dr. Milton W. Hamilton, Assistant State Historian of New York, and Miss Edna Jacobsen, Division of Manuscripts, New York State Library, supplied the original text of the Examination of Stephen Coffin. The Historical Society of Pennsylvania, Richard Norris Williams, 2nd, Director, supplied a number of other items. The Muncy Historical Society, in May, and the Erie County Historical Society, in November, 1953, listened to abbreviated versions of the manuscript for this pamphlet; their questions and comments were very helpful.

This pamphlet could not have been undertaken and published but for the approval and authorization of the Pennsylvania Historical and Museum Commission. In particular, the Honorable Charles G. Webb, chairman of the Commission's historical activities committee, has taken a keen interest in the work from its very beginnings in the cooperative project for the publication of the Contrecoeur Papers, and has been constant in his encouragement. To Dr. Donald A. Cadzow, the Executive Director, and to Dr. S. K. Stevens, State Historian, I am also especially grateful not only for their interest in the work but also for letting me take the time to do it. It should be added, too, that past collaboration with Doctor Stevens in preparing and editing many Commission publications has provided an invaluable guide in the accomplishment of the present task.

DONALD H. KENT

SELECTED BIBLIOGRAPHY

Here are listed only the works and source material which have been most useful, without any attempt at completeness. For a more detailed list, see Fernand Grenier's bibliography in the *Papiers Contrecoeur*.

Archives du Séminaire de Québec: Fonds Viger-Verreau [V-V]
Papiers Contrecoeur (Boxes I to IV)
Papiers Legardeur de Saint-Pierre (Box V)
Papiers Marin (Box V)
> This collection was made by Jacques Viger, first Mayor of the City of Montreal, and by Father Hospice Verreau, who bequeathed it to the Séminaire de Québec. There are microfilm copies in the General Library of the Université Laval, and in the Historical Division of the Pennsylvania Historical and Museum Commission.

Boishébert, Charles Deschamps de, *Mémoire pour le Sieur de Boishébert* . . . Paris, 1763. Transcript in the Public Archives of Canada.

[Bonin, Jolicoeur Charles]. *Travels in New France by J.C.B.*, edited by S. K. Stevens, Donald H. Kent, and Emma Edith Woods. Harrisburg, Pennsylvania Historical Commission, 1941.
> A translation of H. R. Casgrain, ed., *Voyage au Canada dans le nord de l'Amérique septentrionale fait depuis 1751 à 1761 par J.C.B.* Quebec, 1887.

Buck, Solon J. and Elizabeth H., *The Planting of Civilization in Western Pennsylvania*. Pittsburgh, University of Pittsburgh Press, 1939.

Darlington, Mary C., ed., *History of Colonel Henry Bouquet and the Western Frontiers of Pennsylvania*. [Pittsburgh, 1920.]
> This includes Trent's journal, July 11-September 14, 1753.

Darlington, W. M., ed., *Christopher Gist's Journals* . . . Pittsburgh, 1893.

Fitzpatrick, John C., ed., *The Diaries of George Washington, 1748-1799*. Volume I, 1748-1770. New York, Houghton Mifflin, 1925.

Freeman, Douglas Southall, *George Washington: A Biography*. Volumes I-II, Young Washington. New York, Scribners, 1948.

Frégault, Guy, *François Bigot, administrateur français*. 2 vols., Montreal, 1948.
> A translation of Volume II, pages 57-72, appeared as "The Epoch of the Belle Rivière," in *Pennsylvania History*, Vol. XVIII, No. 3, July, 1951, and as a Commission reprint.

Galbreath, C. B., ed., *Expedition of Céloron to the Ohio Country in 1749*. Columbus, Ohio, 1921.
> Contains the journals of Céloron and Father Bonnecamps.

Gipson, Lawrence Henry, *Zones of International Friction: North America South of the Great Lakes Region, 1748-1754.* Volume IV of the series, *The British Empire Before the American Revolution.* New York, Knopf, 1939.

Gosselin, Mgr. Amédée, ed., *Journaux de campagnes de Joseph-Gaspard Chaussegros de Léry* (1749-1759), in RAPQ (1926-1927), pages 331-405.

Grenier, Fernand, ed., *Papiers Contrecoeur et autres documents concernant le conflit anglo-français sur l'Ohio de 1745 à 1756.* Université Laval, Publications des Archives du Séminaire de Québec, I. Quebec, Les Presses Universitaires Laval, 1952.

Kent, Donald H., ed., "Contrecoeur's Copy of George Washington's Journal for 1754," in *Pennsylvania History,* Vol. XIX, No. 1, January, 1952; also a Commission reprint.

Long, M. H., *A History of the Canadian People.* 2 vols., Toronto, 1942.

Margry, Pierre, ed., *Mémoires et documents pour servir à l'histoire des origines françaises des pays d'outremer. Découvertes et établissements des Français dans l'ouest et dans le sud de l'Amérique septentrionale (1679-1754).* 6 vols., Paris, 1879-1888.

Mémoire contenant le Précis des faits, avec leurs pièces justificatives, pour servir de réponse aux OBSERVATIONS envoyées par les Ministres d'Angleterre dans les cours de l'Europe. Paris, 1756.
    Generally attributed to the Duc de Choiseul, it contains the first published version of Washington's journal for 1754. The Commission has a photostatic copy of this from the Historical Society of Pennsylvania.

O'Callaghan, Edmund B., ed., *Documents Relative to the Colonial History of the State of New York.* Volume X. Albany, 1858.

Parkman, Francis, *Montcalm and Wolfe.* 2 vols., Boston, 1926.

Pennsylvania Archives, Second Series, edited by John Blair Linn and William N. Egle. Vol. VI. Papers Relating to the French Occupation in Western Pennsylvania. Harrisburg, 1877.

Pennsylvania Colonial Records: Minutes of the Provincial Council of Pennsylvania, from the Organization to the Termination of the Proprietary Government. 10 vols. Philadelphia, 1851-1852.

Rapport de l'archiviste de la province de Québec. [RAPQ.] Quebec, 1920-   . Edited by Pierre-Georges Roy to 1940, and thereafter by Antoine Roy.
    See especially (1923-1924) for Montcalm and Bougainville *mémoires;* (1924-1925) and (1927-1928) for other important *mémoires;* (1926-1927) for the De Léry journals; (1931-1932), (1932-1933), and (1933-1934) for the La Pause Papers; and (1930-1931) and (1932-1933) for material on French traders in the Ohio country.

Sargent, Winthrop, ed., *The History of an Expedition against Fort Duquesne, in 1755, under Major-General Edward Braddock*. Philadelphia, Lippincott, 1856.

Severance, Frank Hayward, *An Old Frontier of France: The Niagara Region and Adjacent Lakes under French Control*. 2 vols., New York, 1917.

Shortt, Adam, ed., *Documents Relating to Canadian Currency, Exchange, and Finance during the French Period*. 2 vols., Ottawa, 1925.
Useful for its notes on various individuals.

Slick, Sewell Elias, *William Trent and the West*. Harrisburg, Archives Publishing Co., 1947.

Stevens, S. K., and Donald H. Kent, *The Expedition of Baron de Longueuil*. Second edition, Harrisburg, .Pennsylvania Historical Commission, 1941.
Also reissued in abridged form as Historic Pennsylvania Leaflet No. 16. Harrisburg, Pennsylvania Historical and Museum Commission, 1953.

Stevens, S. K., and Donald H. Kent, eds., *Journal of Chaussegros de Léry* [1754-1755]. Harrisburg, Pennsylvania Historical Commission, 1940.

Stevens, S. K., and Donald H. Kent, *Wilderness Chronicles of Northwestern Pennsylvania*. Harrisburg, Pennsylvania Historical Commission, 1941.

Tanguay, Cyprien, *Dictionnaire généalogique des familles canadiennes*. 7 vols., Montreal, 1871-1890.

Trudel, Marcel, "L'affaire Jumonville," in *Revue d'histoire de l'Amérique française*, Vol. VI, No. 3 (December, 1952), pages 331-373.

Wallace, Paul A. W., *Conrad Weiser, 1696-1760, Friend of Colonist and Mohawk*. Philadelphia, University of Pennsylvania Press, 1945.

Wallace, W. Stewart, *The Dictionary of Canadian Biography*. 2 vols., Second Edition, Toronto, 1945.

Winsor, Justin, *Mississippi Basin: The Struggle in America Between England and France, 1697-1763, with Full Cartographical Illustrations from Contemporary Sources*. New York, 1895.

FOR FURTHER READING

This short list of books, prepared for later reprints of *this* book, should assist the reader in further exploring topics that are part of the narrative.

Aquila, Richard. *The Iroquois Restoration: Iroquois Diplomacy on the Colonial Frontier, 1701-1754.* Detroit: Wayne State University Press, 1984.

Bailey, Kenneth P. *Christopher Gist: Colonial Frontiersman, Explorer, and Indian Agent.* Hamden, Conn.: Shoe String Press, 1976.

Bird, Harrison. *Battle for a Continent: The French and Indian War, 1754-1763.* New York: Oxford University Press, 1965.

Cleland, Hugh. *George Washington in the Ohio Valley.* Pittsburgh: University of Pittsburgh Press, 1955.

Fregault, Guy. *Canada: The War of the Conquest.* Toronto: Oxford University Press, 1969.

Hunter, William A. *Forts on the Pennsylvania Frontier, 1753-1758.* Harrisburg: Pennsylvania Historical and Museum Commission, 1960.

Jennings, Francis. *Empire of Fortune: Crowns, Colonies and Tribes in the Seven Years War in America.* New York: W. W. Norton, 1988. Available in paperbound edition.

Kopperman, Paul E. *Braddock at the Monongahela.* Pittsburgh: University of Pittsburgh Press, 1977.

O'Meara, Walter. *Guns at the Forks.* Pittsburgh: University of Pittsburgh Press, 1979. Paperbound reprint.

Schoenfeld, Maxwell P. *Fort de la Presqu'Ile.* Erie: Erie County Historical Society, 1979.

Stotz, Charles Morse. *Outposts of the War for Empire: The French and English in Western Pennsylvania, Their Armies, Their Forts, Their People, 1749-1764.* Pittsburgh: University of Pittsburgh Press, 1985.